kauri

First published in 2004 by New Holland Publishers (NZ) Ltd
Auckland • Sydney • London • Cape Town

218 Lake Road, Northcote, Auckland, New Zealand
Unit 1, 66 Gibbes Street, Chatswood, NSW 2067, Australia
86–88 Edgware Road, London W2 2EA, United Kingdom
80 McKenzie Street, Cape Town 8001, South Africa

www.newhollandpublishers.co.nz

ISBN: 978 1 86966 037 6

Publishing manager: Matt Turner
Commissioned by Renée Lang
Editorial team: Linda Cassells; Brian O'Flaherty
Picture editors: Fionna Campbell; Dee Murch
Designer: Nick Turzynski, redinc.
Maps: Nick Keenleyside

A catalogue record for this book is available from the National Library of New Zealand

10 9 8 7 6 5 4 3 2

Colour reproduction by Microdot, Auckland, New Zealand
Printed in China at Everbest Printing Co Ltd., on paper sourced from sustainable forests

Picture credits

Alexander Turnbull Library (ATL) cover and title page image, p24 (below), p25, p31, p52, p55, p57, p60 (right), p62, p64, p66, p69, p70, p77, p79, p81, p82, p105, p106, p107 (right), p121, p122, p124, p125 (top), p134 (top), p141, p142, p152; **Archives New Zealand** p178; **Auckland City Library** p104, p116, p117 (top), p119 (top right), p130 (top); **Auckland Public Library** p128; **Auckland War Memorial Museum** p16, p68, p91, p107 (left), p108, p110; **Australian War Memorial** p61; **William Coffey** p159; **Department of Conservation (DoC)** p19, p119 (below left) photo: Tony Kellaway, p177, p189, p190; **Don Donovan** p117 (below), p119 (top left); **Rei Hamon** p4, p36; **Matakohe Museum** p37 (right), p84, p88, p89, p90, p93, p96, p97, p99, p100, p101, p102, p111, p113, p125 (below), p126, p127, p130, p134 (below), p139, p143, p145, p162, p171, p179, p180; **Matakohe Museum/ Tudor Collins Collection** p150, p151, p153, p157, p163, p164; **National Archives** p37 (left), p38, p43, p98, p154, p155, p157, p 158, p161; **National Archives/New Zealand Forest Service** p170, p175, p184 (below), p187; **National Archives/State Forest Service** p166, p168, p172; **National Library of Australia (NLofA)** p60 (left); ***New Zealand Herald*** p131; **New Zealand Historic Places Trust** p119 (below right) photo: Belinda Brown; ***Northern Advocate*** p146; **Joanna Orwin** p148; **Photo NZ** p199; **Kevin Prime** p137; **Rob Suisted** p184 (top); **Nancy Tichborne**, from *1000 Years of Gardening in New Zealand*: p28/9; **Time Capsule** University of Auckland: p50; **William Toomath** p118; **Transit NZ** © Stephen King: p192; **Vivian Ward**, from *Prehistoric NZ*: p15; **Waitangi Treaty Grounds** p183; **Cliff Whiting**, courtesy of National Library of New Zealand: p24 (top)

Colour section

Chapter 1: ATL; **Chapter 2**: DoC, DoC, Dick Roberts Photo Library (DR), DR, DoC, DR, DR, DR; **Chapter 3**: ATL, Auckland Art Gallery, ATL; **Chapter 4**: ATL, ATL, NLofA, ATL; **Chapter 5**: ATL, ATL, Omapere Museum, NLofA; **Chapter 6**: ATL, Davies Furniture; **Chapter 9**: DoC, DoC, DoC, DoC, Kauri 2000; **Chapter 10**: Cliff Whiting courtesy of Christchurch Polytech

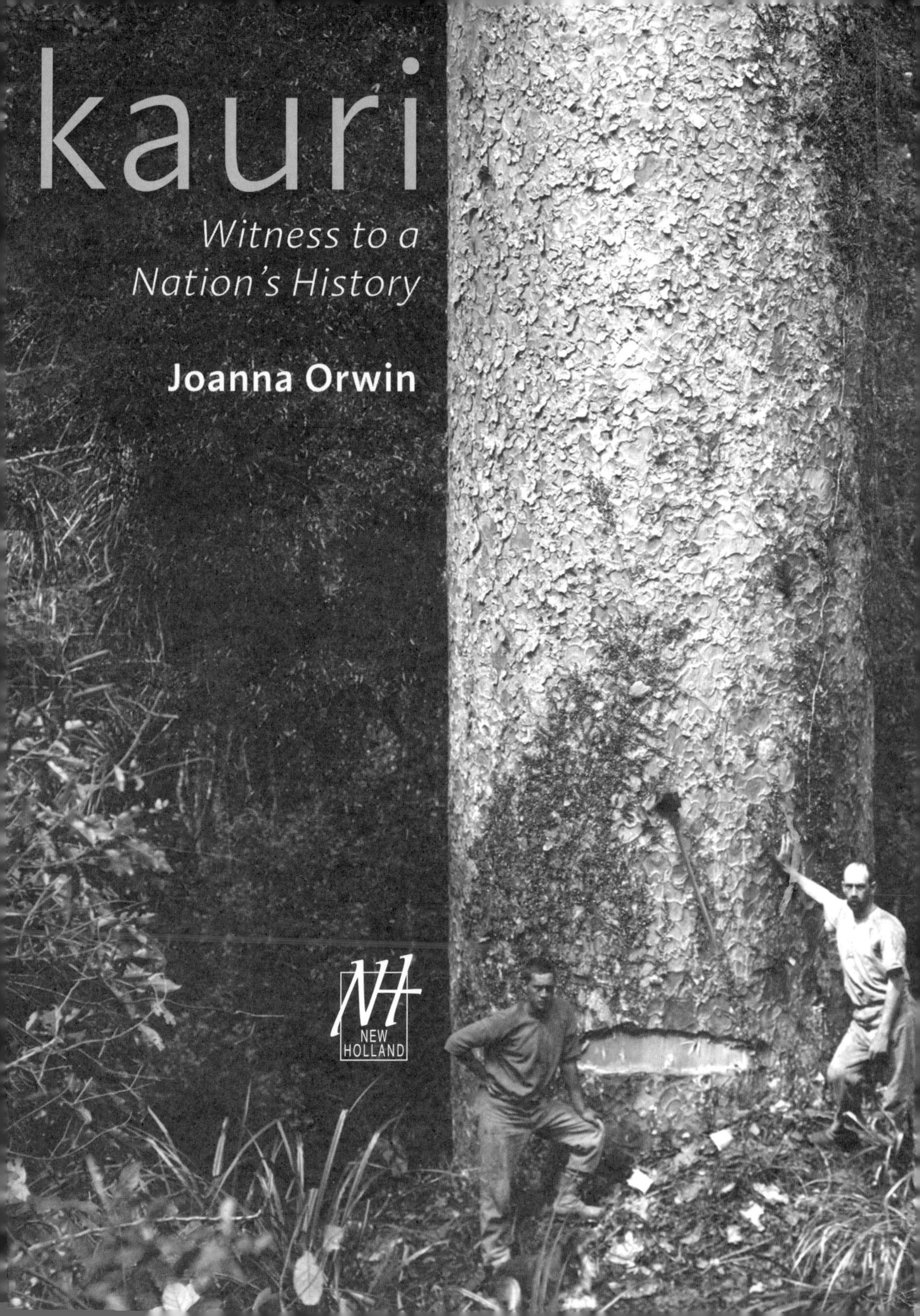
kauri
Witness to a Nation's History
Joanna Orwin
NH
NEW HOLLAND

Contents

Maps

Preface

When New Holland Publishers approached me about writing this book, I immediately thought of the classic books already written by people far more knowledgeable about kauri than I (a mere South Islander) could ever be. The challenge was daunting, but the opportunity to explore an area and subject new to me was irresistible. I set out to find different perspectives and untold stories that would add to existing perceptions of the place of kauri in New Zealand's history. These perspectives and stories inevitably reflect my own interests, the people I met on the journey, and the byways down which they and the research led me. I could not have explored those byways without the generous help of a 2003 Award in History granted by the New Zealand History Research Trust Fund (Te Manatu Taonga/Ministry for Culture and Heritage).

Beyond the well-known but always fascinating history of kauri timber and gum, I gathered material on Maori lifestyles in the kauri region, the role of kauri in early contacts between Maori and Europeans, its later role in the settlement patterns of a new colony, and its impact on trade and a developing economy — from both Maori and Pakeha perspectives. A foray into natural history added present ecological thinking on kauri's place in our remaining natural forests, the growth of New Zealand's conservation movement amid conflicting philosophies on how to preserve and protect what remains of the kauri forests, followed by today's community efforts to restore the surviving kauri forests, set against a background of increasing international obligations for management of native forests.

With a time frame that extended from the arrival of the first Polynesian settlers through to the year of writing (2003), and every turn yielding interesting material, I had to accept that I could not provide an in-depth full regional coverage in a book of this size. Instead, I chose specific themes, then explored each one only in the geographical area that seemed best to illustrate that theme and for which I was able to gather new material. Inevitably, this has mostly come from the main kauri areas — Northland and the Coromandel. Smaller areas like Auckland's Waitakere Ranges and the scattered ranges with kauri south of Auckland, in the Waikato and the Bay of Plenty, I have left to those with detailed local knowledge better able than me to tell their equally rich stories.

Whenever possible, I talked to people with expertise or family stories that would extend the content of the book beyond what I could provide by researching published and archival material alone. These people, their enthusiasm for kauri, and their generosity in sharing their knowledge and stories during taped interviews (in person or by phone) have enriched both this book and me in immeasurable ways. Much of their information and insight appears as verbatim quotes in the text. I am deeply grateful to them all. Kevin Prime (Ngati

Hine) introduced me to the Motatau area (inland Bay of Islands) and its close and continuing involvement with kauri, and has patiently answered my ongoing questions. Erima Henare, Jim Coffey, and the late Prime Cooper gave me glimpses of life in the close-knit Ngati Hine community. John Klaricich, Joey Neill, Bunty Howearth (Nga Puhi) and the late Toi (Hone) Marsden (Ngai Takoto, Muriwhenua, and Nga Puhi) shared stories and information from the Hokianga. Alex Nathan and Gary Hooker (Te Roroa) of Dargaville provided information and perspectives on Waipoua, Hec Busby (Te Rarawa and Ngati Kahu) of Doubtless Bay shared his expertise on building canoes, and Harry Koroneho (Ngati Tamatera) provided some information on the traditional role of kauri on the Coromandel. Margaret Orbell reviewed the chapter on kauri in the Maori world. E nga kaumatua kua haere ki nga tipuna inaianei, ko tenei he poroporoaki atu ki a korua; haere, haere, haere. E koro, e kui, e hoa ma, ka nui aku mihi atu ki a koutou katoa i nga korero, i nga taonga, i nga kete o matauranga. Friends and former colleagues Peter Bellingham and Rob Allen of Landcare Research suggested suitable readings, lent me reference books and papers, and discussed botanical and native forestry issues covered in the chapters on natural history and conservation. John Ogden answered questions about ecology and the University of Auckland's dendrochronology project, and Gretel Boswijk provided photographs. Peter Bellingham and John Ogden reviewed the natural history chapter. Department of Conservation's John Beachman contributed a valuable overview on the changing perspectives of kauri from exploitation to conservation, Piet Nieuwland lent me Department documents and reviewed the final two chapters, and Peter Carter pointed me in appropriate directions for Coromandel information. Graeme Darroch skippered a memorable day on the Hokianga, visiting the sites of Maori skirmishes, mission houses, and kauri mills. Edsel Weber and Kevin Sterling contributed stories and perspectives on the Kaipara. Chris Bergman gave me insight into salvage logging and sustainable harvest. Stephen King shared his experiences of conservation at Waipoua, Rei Hamon his experiences of bush work, art, and conservation on the Coromandel. Gordon Ell gave permission to use information about the kauri national park debate from his taped contribution to the Forest and Bird's Seventy-fifth Anniversary Commemorative Oral Histories. Members of the Yelavich family, Drago, Gojko, Nellie, and Anna, contributed stories of their Dalmatian upbringing on the gum-fields at Ahipara Hill. Milan Jurlina told me about his family's gum-buying business at Sweetwater. John Klaricich (Nga Puhi) of the Hokianga and sisters Mrs Kate Phillips and Mrs Florrie Berghan (Muriwhenua) of the Far North shared family memories of Maori–Dalmatian gum-digging communities. Roy Wagener, Tommy Northwood, and Vic Hensley offered insights and sources for information on the gum days. I acknowledge also the many others who contributed snippets of information about kauri in passing.

This book could not have been written without the solid foundation and direction provided by the research and writings of many people. Their valuable contributions are acknowledged in the references provided for each chapter at the end of the book. While acknowledging the use of their material, I take full responsibility for any errors I have made in factual content or interpretation. Access to published and archival material was greatly helped by the staff of the Macmillan Brown Library, University of Canterbury (in particular, Max Broadbent, Jill Durney, and Christine Bush), the team at the Otamatea Kauri Museum, Matakohe (led by Betty Nelley) — who also helped with picture research — and staff at many small museums throughout the kauri region. Paul Frawley's preliminary search of the New Zealand Forest Service photographic collection made a day at National Archives rewarding, and Ferne McKenzie retrieved suitable illustrations for me from the Department of Conservation photolibrary. I thank Richard King for recommending me as the project's potential author and New Holland's publishing manager Renée Lang for trusting that recommendation. I would not have embarked on this journey without the encouragement of friend and kauri aficionado Lynda Burns and the enduring support I receive from my family — John, Sally, and Kate, and sister Prill, who shared some of my northern explorations. Finally, I thank the team at New Holland Publishers — particularly project manager/editor Linda Cassells, editor Brian O'Flaherty, book designer Nick Turzynski, and publisher's assistant Fionna Campbell — for their support, enthusiasm, and expertise in transforming my manuscript and pile of potential illustrations into this finished book.

The following copyright owners of published material quoted in this book have kindly given their permission: S. M. Mead and the Victoria University Press for use of pepeha 330, 2153, 2154, and 2045 from *Nga Pepeha a nga Tipuna*; Anne Salmond and Penguin Books NZ for material from *Two Worlds* and *Between Worlds*; the Alexander Turnbull Library for extracts from Isobel Ollivier's translations of journals from Marion du Fresne's visit to New Zealand; J. Halkett, E. V. Sale, and Reed Publishing for material from *The World of the Kauri*; the Hokianga Historical Society's Omapere Museum for extracts from their transcription of John Webster's letter books (originals held by the Baker family); W. R. Ryburn for material from *Tall Spars, Steamers and Gum*; P. A. Eaddy and Penguin Books NZ for material from *'Neath Swaying Spars*; J. Webster (editor, *Journal of the Auckland Historical Society*) for extracts from W. A. Bell, 'Life in a Kauri Timber Camp'; A. H. Reed and Reed Publishing for extracts from *The New Story of Kauri*; D. Mackay and R. Murray for extracts from J. Murray's quotes in *Working the Kauri*; and the Sound Archives/Nga Taonga Korero for material from interviews with M. Clotworthy (quoted in *Working the Kauri*) and C. Hovell.

Joanna Orwin, Christchurch

Introduction

In the depths of Northland's Waipoua Forest, the giant kauri Tane Mahuta — lord of the forest — stands alone. His vast trunk separates earth from sky — just as in the Maori legend Tane Mahuta forced the separation of Rangi the sky-father and Papa the earth-mother to bring light to the world at the time of the creation. This ancient tree bears silent witness to a time without people, a time of primeval forests, and the shaping of a landscape. Already a mature tree before the landfall of the first migration canoes from the Pacific, Tane Mahuta has endured throughout the brief human history of a young nation.

The story of Tane Mahuta and the kauri forests that once dominated the northern landscapes of New Zealand is a microcosm of New Zealand's history. This is a story of the earliest inhabitants and the development of their lifestyle and mythology. It is a story of the first encounters between two peoples with markedly different world views and cultures — differences that still affect us today. It is a story of Maori chiefs and warriors, of European sailors and explorers, missionaries and traders, bushmen and pioneers, migrant communities and entrepreneurs — a mix that underlies New Zealand's emerging national identity. The story of kauri runs parallel to the story of a new colony's developing economy and society, the establishment of New Zealand's first seat of government, and the growth of its first city. Rising above this human history is the continuing story of the tree itself, the kauri. For it was the ruthless destruction of kauri forests over more than 100 years that led to the first efforts to protect some of New Zealand's rapidly dwindling native forests and to the growth of the conservation movement in the mid-twentieth century. Now, in the twenty-first century, the kauri has become an icon; the surviving giant trees are protected and have become revered, the subject of pilgrimage and tourist awe.

The northern region of New Zealand can be seen as the cradle of the country's human history — both Maori and Pakeha. This region supported a large Maori population in the years before European contact, and still does. It was most likely here that migrating Polynesians established their first permanent foothold, adapting their lifestyle to the climate and the resources of the coast and kauri forest. As they adapted, they developed a rich body of legend, lore, and legacy around the new landscape and its giant kauri trees. As the population grew, competition over status and dwindling resources escalated. Gradually more clearly defined alliances evolved among related groups of people. These groups kept moving across the landscape, harvesting resources or engaging in tribal warfare. Their fluctuating fortunes had created a pattern of intermittently abandoned settlements and fortifications by the time the first European ships ventured into Northland waters in the late eighteenth century.

Europeans were first drawn to northern New Zealand by rumours of trees suitable for the spars of sailing ships. Soon they realised that the light yet strong timber of kauri was ideal. They negotiated with local Maori, mostly by sign language, over kauri timber and provisions. These early contacts between the two peoples were often volatile. Within a few years of being exposed to the novel concept of a world beyond their own, northern Maori were venturing across the oceans to experience it for themselves, some meeting colonial governors and kings with considerable aplomb. Quick to seize opportunities and turn the unfamiliar to their own advantage, Maori became astute traders and entrepreneurs. It was on Maori that the new European arrivals depended for support and supplies. In turn, Maori bartered pigs and potatoes as well as flax and kauri spars for the trade goods and muskets that gave them the edge in competitive tribal relationships.

For more than a century, the extraction of kauri — the largest timber tree by volume in the world — strongly influenced early European exploration, settlement patterns, and commercial development in the north. It was trade in kauri timber and gum (kauri resin was first used in varnish) that made Auckland the most populated province in early colonial New Zealand. When the new colony's capital shifted from Kororareka (now Russell) in the Bay of Islands to Auckland in 1840, the city's growth — both its buildings and its industry — was based on kauri. By the late nineteenth century, hundreds of ships were loading cargoes of kauri timber and gum for a thriving export trade.

By the end of the nineteenth century, the vast resource of the kauri forests had almost vanished. Timber and timber rights were sold cheaply in a government push to encourage the clearing of land acquired from Maori for pastoral farming. Logging was often followed by burning, both accidental and deliberate. Many European settlers on newly cleared land paid for their farms by digging and selling kauri gum, an industry that matched the export value of kauri timber. Local Maori and migrants from the Austrian empire, mainly Dalmatians, were the backbone of the gum industry, but it also attracted itinerants and unemployed men from the growing urban settlements further south. The kauri gum and timber industries fostered workers whose values came to be seen as typical of the New Zealander — tough, enterprising, practical, and hardworking.

The story of kauri came full circle in the twentieth century, from exploitation and destruction to preservation and restoration, and ultimately to the renewal of some of the respect accorded kauri in the first era of human settlement. Increasing concern about the loss of the forests had been expressed at official levels for some decades, with little result. It took the dedication of a few determined citizens to gain a reprieve for the remaining kauri forests. Polarised philosophies of conservation, management, and restoration of the kauri forests continued to be the source of controversy to the end of the century and beyond.

Now, in the twenty-first century, the conflicting demands of protection and use still pose problems. Invading weeds and pests threaten the health and biodiversity of the remaining kauri forests. In a country endowed with national parks, kauri forests are still not represented — an ongoing source of debate. Waipoua Forest, home of Tane Mahuta, is subject to a long-standing claim before the Waitangi Tribunal that raises issues of land ownership and traditional rights. At the same time, Maori and Pakeha communities are now actively involved in the conservation management of the remaining kauri forests. International agreements on biodiversity, ecologically sustainable management of forest resources, and reduction of carbon emissions present obligations and opportunities that may shape the future of kauri. Throughout history, the story of kauri has reflected and encapsulated the story of New Zealand. It continues to do so in a modern world.

CHAPTER 1

Father of the forest — te matua o te wao

KAURI IN THE MAORI WORLD

A new land

Raucous seabirds wheel overhead. Scanning the horizon for other hints of land, the Polynesian voyagers spot a distant band of cloud. Their double-hulled sailing canoe now approaches a land mass larger than any they have known before. A day or so later, they stumble ashore, stretching legs that are cramped from several weeks at sea on a voyage that may have taken them 3000 kilometres or more from home. Beyond this coastline, as far as the voyagers can see, forest covers the rugged landscape, cloaking both low and high land in dense greenery that fades to blue on the distant mountains. No one is there to greet them.

The Polynesian voyagers probably sailed to New Zealand in double-hulled canoes similar to this one sketched in the Pacific by Webber, an artist on Cook's third voyage in 1776–1780. This canoe has been estimated as twenty-nine metres long.

This Ngati Whatua figurehead was carved in the Kaipara in 1882 for *Taheretikitiki*, a canoe made from a large kauri felled near Waimauku for Paora Tuhaere of Orakei.

The exact place of this first landing in New Zealand is not known, but our knowledge of the prevailing winds and currents suggests that it was probably somewhere on the east coast. The exact timing of the landing is still a matter of debate, but archaeological evidence suggests that settlements were well established in the thirteenth century on the coasts of both the North and South Islands, so this first landing may have been in the late eleventh or early twelfth century. Some believe it to have been much earlier, but so far there is not enough reliable evidence to support this. Nor do we know the exact point of departure, but we can be certain the people were East Polynesian. The number of people, canoes, and landings is also not known exactly, but their journey had been carefully planned — women as well as men were on board, and they had with them some domestic animals and plants. These were people in search of new land to settle.

New Zealand was the last and most distant outpost to be settled by sea-faring people in a sequence of exploration and settlement that had spread out from Melanesia across the entire Pacific over a period of 4000 years or more. Armed with traditional knowledge, navigational and maritime expertise, and survival skills developed over many generations, the voyagers were also protected by the powerful rituals of their culture. They were well equipped physically and mentally to survive a voyage that was longer in distance and time than any other their people had undertaken.

Not all the animals and plants likely to have been on board survived. Dogs and rats did, but any chickens and pigs they brought with them did not. No matter, the new land was well stocked with excellent meat supplies. Fur seals and other sea mammals proved obligingly susceptible to a swift blow from a club. Some areas sported extraordinarily large flightless birds, which were promptly called chickens — moa — no doubt with tongue in cheek. Of the plants they brought with them, only kumara and gourd could be grown as far south as Banks Peninsula. The less hardy taro, yam, paper mulberry (its bark used to make tapa cloth) and a tropical cabbage tree survived and thrived only in the northern third of the North Island — the subtropical region where kauri forests dominated. Northern New Zealand was therefore the most likely region of early permanent settlement.

Taking stock

Experimentation and adaptation were key to survival in this new land. Despite its latitude and cooler climate, much about the land was familiar to these early Polynesian settlers. Many plants in the northern subtropical kauri forests looked familiar enough for most of their experimentation in food gathering to succeed — knowledge of wild 'famine foods' was an essential part of the Polynesian survival kit. Such plants were named after relatives or look-alikes from home. Localised sources of familiar stones like basalt and obsidian were exploited for tools from the time of arrival. They were soon joined by less familiar local stones like chert and argillite that responded to traditional manufacturing techniques. Timber trees like kauri and totara had familiar characteristics that could be put to the test.

At the same time, the voyagers adapted their oral traditions, myths, and legends to the new landscape. Legends evolved about ancestors with supernatural powers who had sailed their founding canoes along the coasts, shaping and naming the landscape to make the place suitable for settling. As the generations passed, local versions of traditional stories reinforced ties with the land that became known as Aotearoa.

One such Northland story attributes the pre-human destruction of an ancient kauri forest to Kupe, said to be the first person to sail to New Zealand and prepare the way for those who followed. In many Nga Puhi traditions, Kupe returned to the place of origin, Hawaiki, from the Hokianga Harbour after circumnavigating the North Island. When people settled in the Hokianga, fire-blackened kauri roots and stumps were often exposed beneath the drifting sand dunes of North Head. According to John Klaricich (Nga Puhi), the Hokianga story says that when Kupe was ready to leave for Hawaiki, he thrust a burning stake, Te Pouahu, into the ground on North Head to serve as a beacon for those who would follow him. After he sailed away, embers from the beacon set the forest alight, destroying it for all time.

With the exception of Kupe, return voyages to the place of origin were unlikely because of the distance and the contrary currents. Over the generations, as the people adapted their lifestyle to the changing challenges of the new land, a distinctive culture slowly emerged.

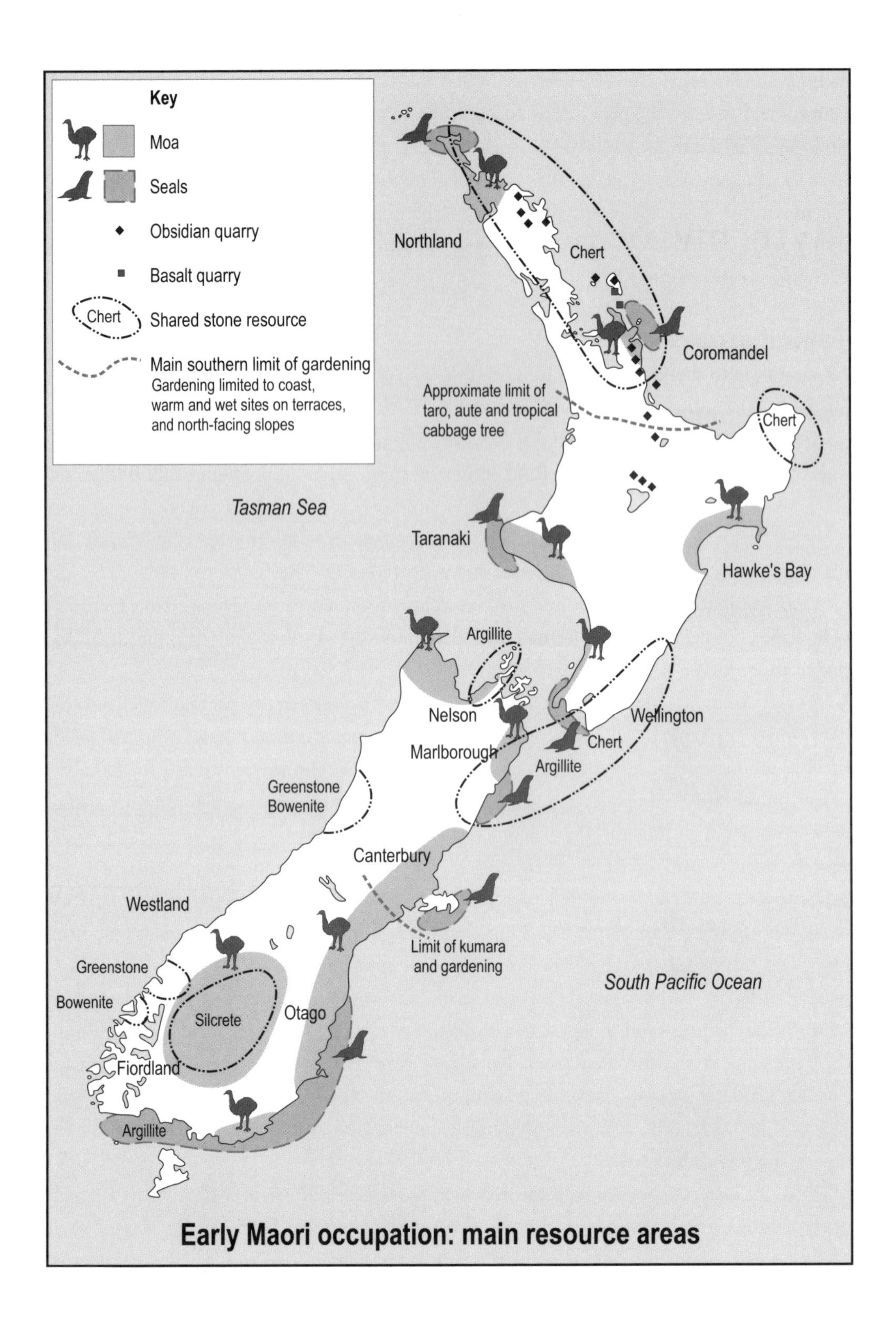

Early Maori occupation: main resource areas

Polynesians became Maori (though they were not to call themselves that until nearly a century after first contact with Europeans), and Aotearoa became the centre of their world and their traditions.

Myth, mystery, and mischief

First and foremost among any society's traditions is the story of creation. Maori versions of the Pacific-wide story became firmly linked to the new land. And so for some Northland peoples it was the giant kauri tree, towering above the canopy of the forest, that brought light and life to the world.

In Te Roroa tradition, the towering trunks of kauri separated earth from sky.

Letting in the light

At the beginning of time, all was darkness. The parents of creation, Rangi the sky-father and Papa the earth-mother, clung together, their sons trapped in darkness between them. Endless time passed before the sons, desperate for light and space, agreed to separate their parents. All but the dissenting Tawhirimatea tried in turn to pry apart the sky and the earth. All failed. Then the strongest of them, Tane Mahuta, pressed his shoulders against his mother Papa and thrust upwards with his powerful legs. Ignoring the protests of his weeping parents as they were torn apart, Tane Mahuta pushed upwards until his father Rangi was forced far up into the sky. Relentless, Tane Mahuta held him there, at last letting in the light.

In the tradition of the Te Roroa people of Waipoua Forest, Tane Mahuta's legs were the massive trunks of giant kauri trees. It was the kauri that succeeded in separating the sky from the earth and in letting in the light that enabled the first springing of life.

Angered by Tane Mahuta's success, Tawhirimatea followed his father Rangi skywards. From there he unleashed his turbulent children — the winds — on his brothers below. Fleeing from his anger, one brother, Tangaroa, took refuge in the sea with his fish children, separating them from Tane Mahuta's children — the plants and creatures of the forest. Then Tu, who represented humans, took revenge against his brothers on the earth and in the sea, seeking out and eating their offspring as food.

As well as fathering plants and creatures, Tane Mahuta fathered the human race by forming the first woman, Hineahuone, from earth, and mating with her. In the Te Roroa version of this story, the kauri links Tane Mahuta's non-human and human children, signifying the interdependence of all living things. Gary Hooker (Te Roroa) says that on a day when the forest is brimming with life, Te Roroa elders would remark: 'Te matua ka kata!' (Our parent — the giant kauri — is laughing!)

This creation story explained the origin and nature of the Maori world. It underlined the kinship or connection between all living things and explained the source of conflict, both natural and human. It identified the fundamental relationship between men and women, men having the specialised sacred role of Rangi the sky-father and women the more pragmatic nurturing role of Papa the earth-mother. Closely associated with these complementary roles was the interaction of two equally complementary states of being — tapu (sacred, restricted, or forbidden) and noa (profane, everyday, ordinary). These states applied to people, things, places, and actions, shaping both religious belief and daily behaviour. In general (and at the risk of over-simplifying a complex world view), men, their activities, and the places they did them were tapu and high status; women and their activities were noa and low status. Interaction and balance between tapu and noa underlay all action in Maori society. Kinship — genealogy or whakapapa — which identified how people, ancestors, and gods were connected, underlay all relationships.

The sacred forest of Tane

The tallest and most valued trees of the forest were treated like chiefs as they were seen as having high status (mana). In particular, kauri, totara, kahikatea, and rata were often given chiefly status. According to Kevin Prime (Ngati Hine), giant kauri would have superseded all others in status in Northland because of their size. Such trees, too large to be of any practical use, were in some areas given godly status, as John Klaricich explains:

> *In the Hokianga, kauri was seen as a timber of prestige and rarely used. It was held in awe and best left alone. It belonged where it was standing, not lying on the ground. Dealing with it required special expertise.*

Any chief-like tree about to be felled for an equally high-status purpose — such as the infrequent making of a large war canoe — would be approached with the caution and respectful ceremony that befitted an elder relative.

Conversely, leading Maori chiefs were often likened to such trees, particularly at their death. Te Heuheu Tukino lamented for his brother killed by Te Atiawa of Taranaki, paying tribute to the enemy with the words: 'Nga tai whakarewa kauri ki te uru' — the kauri-bearing tides of the west. In Northland, kauri replaced totara in the saying: 'Kua hinga te kauri o te wao nui a Tane' (the kauri has fallen in the sacred forest of Tane). Like many Maori sayings, the truth of the natural world lies behind the poetry. When a great tree falls, it often takes lesser trees with it, but at the same time the gap created lets in light, allowing a new generation to spring up, nurtured by the nutrients released by the fallen tree — linking the person who has died to Tane's life-giving work. Kauri was used to acknowledge the death of significant Northland people up to recent times, although Kevin Prime says that the comparison nowadays is often to kahikatea because of its greater dominance in the modern landscape.

Kauri forests themselves were sometimes places of mystery and spiritual significance. Even today, some Maori are reluctant to travel through Waipoua Forest at night. Steep bluffs in the forest house burial caves where the presence of the ancestors is still strong. Toi Marsden (Ngai Takoto, Muriwhenua, and Nga Puhi) has felt that presence:

> *I was going through Waipoua Forest, going through to Auckland by myself. All of a sudden my vehicle cut out, no power, no lights. So I decided to wait until morning to see what was wrong. Just before I dozed off, I could hear these voices. But they were foreign, partly Maori and partly something else. Vague voices. Next thing I woke up and it was broad daylight. Switched the key on and nothing wrong — the vehicle started straight away. Then I looked up and I knew*

exactly where I was. Just up from there are some burial caves, and I thought to myself, that's what it was. They were lonely.

In some forests, the layer formed high above the canopy by the crowns of mature kauri was the home of patupaiarehe or turehu, fairy creatures that elsewhere inhabited mist-shrouded mountains. Human in form, pale-skinned, and often red-haired, turehu had a predilection for human women, either capturing them or coming to them at night — an unexplained pregnancy proof of such a visit. Bunty Howearth (Nga Puhi) retells her great-grandmother's cautionary tale of the dangers of turehu lurking in the mist on the Hokianga beaches:

Engulfed by such a mist, Maramatangi was abducted by Waihoro, a turehu, and taken to his home high in a kauri tree. Homesick, Maramatangi eventually escaped, but her turehu lover continued to visit her at night. Over the years she had five red-haired green-eyed children.

Toi Marsden tells a story that is even closer to home:

Those patupaiarehe or turehu live in the tops of kauri trees in Waipoua and the Waitakere Ranges. I can tell you a story about those turehu that involves my family. My grandmother was living in the Waipoua Forest at the time — as a young woman she went missing for four months. She was quite thin when she came out of the forest, and had lost her Maori language — she'd been brainwashed by those turehu people. It took her nearly two years before she could speak Maori again. She was unlucky — she had red hair and blue eyes, very fair. That's what attracted those turehu people. This was well over 100 years ago; she died in 1882.

The kauri itself could have supernatural powers. Prime Cooper (Ngati Hine) tells of a famous water creature or taniwha, Rangiriri, who lives in the Northern Wairoa River on the Kaipara. It takes the form of a huge semi-submerged kauri log that to this day can be seen travelling against the tide, moving up or down stream.

Forays into the forest

As well as having spiritual and cultural significance, the northern kauri forests were visited by Maori at certain times to obtain timber and gather forest foods to supplement supplies from fishing and gardening.

Treasured trees

Of the great trees of the forest, the ones accorded most value — beyond chiefly status — were those that had multiple uses. Totara was tops. It not only provided superior timber for canoes, houses, and carvings, but its berries also attracted birds, making them susceptible to hunters. Stripped totara bark made convenient containers for storing birds preserved in their own fat. As bird-feeding trees, kahikatea and miro also came high in the economic stakes. Kevin Prime explains that kauri barely featured as a valued resource, despite its grandeur and its excellent timber. Because kauri did not have seed that fed the birds, it did not feed the people. As a result, to most Maori people kauri would not have been seen as a major economic resource, as the use of the forest centred around food gathering.

In the Hokianga, the essential forest resources were manuka and miro, followed by karaka, then akeake. All were used for some or all of the following purposes — food, medicine, shelter, firewood, and wood for weapons or tools. John Klaricich recalls how his mother and her parents were more concerned about land clearances that took the miro away than they were about kauri, as miro was the food tree for pigeons (kukupa).

Harry Koroneho (Ngati Tamatera) says that his people on the Coromandel did consider kauri had some use as a bird tree as it was used as a perch. But in general, Ngati Tamatera saw kauri as trees to be avoided, sometimes using their crowns as a repository for the bones of the dead — a highly tapu function.

In general, even the lesser trees in the forest had more economic value than kauri. In the Hokianga, thin whippy tanekaha saplings were favoured over kauri saplings for fishing rods (matira) for rock-cod fishing. Tanekaha had a lot of uses: timber for paddles and carved pou or house posts, bark for medicines and dyes (sunset reds for cloak borders). John Klaricich recalls:

> *Our people saw tanekaha as more adaptable. It wasn't any more readily available or accessible than kauri because you often had to pass through tanekaha to reach the threshold for kauri trees.*

Lesser berry-producing trees like hinau and taraire that fed the birds were also of more significance than kauri — Kevin Prime says that the birds could eat their leaves as well when food was scarce, but they could not eat kauri leaves.

Kauri gum or kapia had more value in the home than kauri timber, which was no use as firewood, burning with a cold sooty flame. Lumps of the inflammable gum were used as fire starters and were tucked into ti-kouka torches as they burnt with a bright light. Burning gum helped attract eels and other fish, and repelled the insects that damaged

Te Wehenga o Rangi raua ko Papa — this representation of the separation of Rangi and Papa combines carving, painting, and weaving. Designed and created by a group working under the direction of artist Cliff Whiting, it shows Tane Mahuta as he thrusts his parents apart with his legs.

kumara plantations. Soft fresh gum was chewed both as a treatment for stomach upsets and as a tooth cleanser. Kevin Prime remembers chewing it as a child:

> *It was hard work chewing that. When we had toothache, my Mum would add tanekaha sap from under the bark — that had a numbing effect. The sap was probably more effective on its own, but it tasted very bitter.*

A higher-status use of kauri gum was in providing a blue-black pigment for tattooing and paint. 'He kiri wai-kauri' complimented someone with 'a finely tattooed skin', according

Burnt kauri gum yielded a blue-black soot used for tattooing. These chiefs with different styles of facial tattoo (moko) were sketched by Sydney Parkinson during Cook's first voyage in 1768–1771.

to Gary Hooker. Kauri gum was burnt and the soot collected on the underside of leaves or flat pieces of wood. This kauri soot was sometimes buried for years to improve its quality. This gave rise to two other sayings: 'Puritia to ngarahu kauri' and 'Puritia to kauri hei o matenga mou' ('Keep your kauri resin soot' and 'Keep your kauri resin for your death journey'), both of which were applied to a mean or stingy person who had refused to oblige a request for something. More appropriate and generous was the Te Roroa practice at Waipoua that Gary Hooker relates, where caches of kauri soot were kept near known kokowai (red ochre) sources so that approaching visitors could smarten up before being welcomed by their hosts. Soot was also collected by burning kauri and rimu heartwood, then mixing it with shark oil to make black paint for timber, particularly for canoes.

A timber of prestige

Where kauri came into its own was in providing straight-grained light timber that was ideal for canoes. Many of the large highly decorated war canoes described by early Europeans in the Bay of Islands were made from kauri logs. But even in the kauri region, not all canoes were made from kauri. Totara was the preferred timber for carving and canoes, perhaps giving rise to the saying of someone dissatisfied that someone else had gained a hoped-for opportunity: 'He aha i kiia ai ko koe hai totara haere wa, ko au hai kauri tu i te wao?' (Why is it said that you are a totara to go places, while I am a kauri that stands in the forest?) — totara (canoes) took part in high-status exploits, kauri stayed at home producing resin. John Klaricich says that in the Hokianga, totara was always used for small single-hulled canoes, although kauri would have been used for the large war canoes. Harry

Large highly decorated war canoes were symbols of high status. This canoe and its crew were sketched by Sydney Parkinson during Cook's first voyage in 1768–1771. In the north, many such canoes were built from kauri.

Koroneho says that on the Coromandel, Ngati Tamatera apparently did not use kauri timber for canoes or any other purpose.

Kauri being felled for large canoes were selected for their timber attributes rather than ease of extraction. The time taken to haul the logs out was unlikely to be a consideration for workers not on hourly rates. In 1772, Bay of Islands Maori guided Marc-Joseph Marion du Fresne's men to the site where they had extracted kauri for a canoe admired by the French — five kilometres inland through swamp and up and down hills. The French took over two weeks using block and tackle to drag two kauri logs from the same area to within sight of the sea (see Chapter 3, Masts and massacres). The best kauri for war canoes was that growing on the western sides of ridges, according to Hekenukumai (Hec) Busby (Te Rarawa and Ngati Kahu). He says Taupuhi Eruera (one of the experts involved with making the Waitangi canoe in 1940) told him that:

> *During the winter months, the west side of those trees would be hit by the prevailing westerly winds and storms — that made the wood stronger; that side grows slower. The eastern side is the sappy side. When you knock the trees over, the heart is not in the centre, it's closer to the west. That's the heavier wood, so it goes to the bottom of the canoe for stability. To prove that, you put the log in a stream and it will roll over until the heavy side is underneath.*

In the Hokianga, large canoes always had composite hulls made from pieces from several trees — they were not hollowed out from single trees, according to John Klaricich's mother. The bow piece was always made from the root section of the tree, where the multiple grain protected it from splitting. Later, bushmen would observe that kauri timber from stumps was tough and curly. The Waitangi canoe was made from two kauri trees felled in Puketi Forest, one tree for the middle section, another for the two end sections. A third was felled from Tutamoe for the top strakes (planking that increases the canoe's freeboard). It is possible that large canoes were not always made from standing trees, as John believes his mother's information implied that fallen trees were used. Certainly, fallen trees were used for other purposes — he has retrieved half-finished pou (house post) carvings up to 2.5 metres long that had been worked from what appeared to be flood-eroded tanekaha trunks with the roots still attached.

Canoe-making may have been an infrequent event in the daily round, but canoes were always an integral part of Maori life. The heavily indented coastline of the two narrow main islands was over 6000 kilometres long. With a hinterland that was densely forested at the time of first settlement, travel by sea was by far the best option for an ocean-going people used to island-hopping. Canoes had allowed rapid exploration and linked the best settlement sites to essential resources. Up until the late nineteenth century, canoes continued to sustain the contact, connection, and conflict characteristic of the mobile Maori society that developed in Aotearoa.

A changing lifestyle

At first, the Polynesian arrivals chose settlement sites on the east coast with access to sheltered fishing waters — harbours, estuaries, or river mouths (particularly in the South Island), a stable supply of meat (mostly fur seals, sometimes moa, and, if they were lucky, both), and stone resources (stone and adze blanks or blocks were exchanged over long distances). Wherever possible, soils suitable for gardening were also taken into consideration when seeking out settlement sites, but south of Banks Peninsula gardening did not feature. Distinctive regional lifestyles soon developed.

Even in the Far North, gardening would never be as dominant as it had been in tropical Polynesia. In New Zealand's temperate climate, tropical root crops could not yield year-round food supplies — the persistence with gardening probably reflected its cultural importance more than its contribution to the store cupboard. Gardening became but one activity for a people who were forced to move from one resource to another in an energetic and wide-ranging cycle of exploiting and preserving seasonally available foods. The earliest sites examined by archaeologists suggest that the Polynesian pattern of shifting cultivation based on permanent settlements was replaced by a pattern of scattered small settlements (based on a few closely related households) that were often occupied only seasonally.

Despite their small founding population, the Polynesian arrivals had a dramatic impact on an environment that had evolved in the absence of humans. The forests were slow to recover from the traditional practice of burning to clear land for gardens, settlement sites, and access to the interior. Land left fallow after gardening soon became infested with bracken. Bracken root (aruhe) itself became a staple food, but repeated burnings to encourage it made the soil unsuitable for kumara. People cleared new forest land rather than attempting to eradicate bracken on old garden sites. As the population grew and the use of favoured sites became more intensive, the loss of forest led to erosion. By about the fifteenth century, nearly half the original forest had disappeared, some eroded sites had become uninhabitable, and gardening had become more difficult. At the same time, the apparently ample supplies of meat had succumbed to over-exploitation. More than thirty species of birds had become extinct — including all the moa — and the seal colonies had retreated to the far south. The cupboard had become alarmingly bare.

By the fifteenth century, gardening efforts had intensified on the fertile volcanic soils of Northland and Auckland. This reconstruction shows stone mounds being built to grow kumara in neatly laid-out gardens near a fortified Auckland volcano.

Cooperation and competition

As the major meat supplies disappeared, the already highly mobile people migrated inland to unpopulated areas in search of new resources. The seasonal cycle of harvesting, processing, and preserving foods from coast and forest intensified and became more sophisticated. The enforced focus on smaller fry — both fish and fowl — required greater cooperation in order to obtain enough to feed everyone, let alone create any surpluses for displays of wealth and gift exchange. Cooperative ventures encouraged more cohesive groupings that were based on kinship ties. These groupings fluctuated in size and over time, depending on economic and social demands.

Within such kinship groupings, scarce resources were allocated to individuals and families in a more formal way. Boundaries were often signalled by rahui posts — and trespass against the ensuing tapu would result in metaphysical or physical punishment. Rights to such resources were passed down the generations and jealously guarded. In the inland forested valleys of Waipoua for instance, Te Roroa families claimed traditional rights to cultivations, bird trees, rat runs, and bird 'landings' or wharekiri. These named clearings in the kauri forest were maintained by burning to create open areas for hunting kiwi or pigeon. Waipoua resident conservationist Stephen King explains that one such clearing in Waipoua Forest can still be seen at the beginning of the walk to several giant kauri. As a result of generations of occupation and use, much of Waipoua Forest today is secondary growth, and the area preserves some of the most extensive stone-walled cultivation and ritual sites ever found.

Throughout the country, gardening efforts intensified anywhere that kumara growing was possible. In Northland, gardeners focused their efforts on patches of fertile volcanic soils. Associated volcanic cones of the inland Bay of Islands and the Tamaki Isthmus (Auckland) became extensively terraced, with gardens and storage pits on lower levels, settlements on higher levels. Both areas supported increasing populations after the fifteenth century, and the original kauri forests were largely replaced by a patchwork of intensive cultivations and bracken-infested scrubland.

As populations increased, competition for the most favourable sites and resources intensified — an increasing cause of rivalry in a society where any status conferred by birth needed substantiating by action. Polynesians had always been quarrelsome, and there is no reason to assume that feuding subsided in New Zealand. Larger settlements and the growing scale of some cooperative seasonal or occasional ventures (such as making a large canoe, making and fishing with seine nets, expeditions to the interior for pigeons, or large-scale gardening) were accompanied by a growing need to protect the resulting material assets and the hard-gained food supplies from competing rival groups.

Competition and rivalry were founded in status and the need to reciprocate both insult and generosity. After the fifteenth century, the scale of such rivalry seems to have been inflated

After the fifteenth century, defendable locations like these hill tops were fortified as strategic retreats for the people from settlements like the one beside this river, sketched in the Bay of Islands about 1835.

— perhaps by the demands of the new economics and the associated reinforced kinship ties and allegiances. Parts of some settlements became fortified. Elsewhere, pa were built as strategic and defendable retreats on coastal promontories and the rims of already settled volcanic cones. The rapid proliferation of fortified settlements went far beyond the numbers needed for defending food supplies and garden lands. The possession of such conspicuous status symbols also reflected escalating 'one-upmanship' between competing chiefs. Nowhere was this more evident than in the northern region, where settlement was at its densest.

After the fifteenth century, distinctive tribal groups started to evolve as a result of coalescing allegiances that satisfied the demands of status and rivalry. These groups were combinations of related hapu or sub-tribes rather than the iwi of the late nineteenth century. In a land where population was not impeded by space, the response to attack was often to move temporarily or permanently. In some places and at some times, mobility expanded to migration — winning alliances moved onto desirable land and the defeated moved out. In other places, people continued to occupy their territories for generations — newcomers being absorbed by marriage rather than mayhem. By 1750, the mix of change and continuity had created a fluid pattern of occupied and abandoned settlements and fortified pa that shifted across the landscape in response to seasonal activities and fluctuating tribal fortunes.

THE KAURI AND THE WHALE

The whale once said to the kauri, 'Come out to sea with me!'

The kauri replied, 'The sea is not for me. I much prefer my own place.'

The whale said, 'We should swap skins, because you are in danger of being cut down by man and made into a canoe.'

So the whale and the kauri swapped skins. That is why the bark of the kauri is flaky, thin, and full of resin — just as the whale is full of oil. (Taylor 1870)

TE TUMUTUMU AND THE POACHER'S TONGUE

(as told by Kevin Prime)

This is a story about a large kauri stump in the Motatau Valley, inland Bay of Islands. A poacher once had his tongue gouged out and stuck on that stump, 250 or so years ago. That place was called Te Tumutumu, the stump. What the kauri tree was used for is not recorded, but it had been felled in one of the tribal whare wananga sites (tapu places of learning). One of the chiefs of that time, Moeahu, had a kiwi reserve, Te Rahui Kiwi a Moeahu, and this man was caught poaching there.

Moeahu's warriors tracked the poacher all night, each close encounter giving rise to a local place name still used today. They eventually caught him and took him up the valley to where this kauri stump was, gouged out his tongue, and stuck it to the stump. No one else ever stole kiwi from that reserve. This story was told and retold as a deterrent against poaching.

Place names from the story (Translation in italics)

Ahikiwi, the place from where the warriors saw smoke from the poacher's *fire cooking the kiwi*.

Wahapako, *the sound of* the poacher *licking* his *chops*.

Hihaere, *fishing* (for eels) *as he went*.

Waimahaehae, *scrabbling in clear water* (for freshwater mussels and crayfish).

Mautata, where the warriors *almost caught* him.

Horahora, where he *spread out* his wet clothes to dry after crossing a stream.

Katakawaro (ka-taka-te-waro), where he left his ti kouka torch and *a burning ember fell off*.

Tororoa, the *huge conflagration* where the valley burnt.

Whakakiore, where he had crawled through the undergrowth, *acting like a rat*.

Otukaiao, the mound *where he stood inhaling the new dawn*.

Te Tumutumu, where they gouged out his tongue and stuck it in *the* kauri *stump*.

Waeweriweri, where they hung him up by one *leg* until it *rotted*.

CHAPTER 2

Legends in the landscape

HOW AND WHERE KAURI GROW

Kauri, king of kings

The first glimpse of a towering wall beyond a screen of leaves. Anticipation mingles with disbelief. A few metres further along the path, Tane Mahuta comes into full view. Framed by the tracery of tree ferns and a wealth of texture and shape in every shade of green, the trunk of the largest living New Zealand kauri soars skywards. With a girth of nearly fourteen metres, this huge tree rises without tapering for nearly eighteen metres. Like all kauri, its clean ash-grey bark is unencumbered by branch, fern, liane, or perching plant. On a damp dull day, light reflects from the trunk, giving the tree a mystic aura.

Slowly the eye is drawn upwards to the first ring of massive branches that support the crown. Beyond this ring, the crown rises close to another thirty-five metres, so that the tree's total height reaches more than fifty metres. Immense and spreading, the crown forms an umbrella over the main canopy of the forest below. Tane Mahuta still thrusts the sky high above the roof of the forest, separating earth from sky, as in the ancient Maori legend.

Aging gracefully

Tane Mahuta is one of the last of the recorded giant kauri trees still standing. It is the most accessible giant, only a few minutes' walk from the highway that runs through Waipoua Forest. With the second largest living kauri, Te Matua Ngahere, a few kilometres away, visitors to the forest can walk beneath trees that have been mature for over 1000 years and are thought to be 1500–2000 years old. Although even larger kauri were recorded in the past, giant trees were always exceptional. Only a scattered few specimens ever reached this size or age.

It has been claimed that some kauri were up to 4000 years of age, such as the largest kauri ever officially measured — Kairaru, with a girth of twenty metres and height to first branch of thirty metres, which was destroyed by fire on Tutamoe Mountain near Dargaville before the end of the nineteenth century. Many such claims were based on extrapolations from girth, but these extrapolations have proved inaccurate because growth rates vary according to the site and over the life of a tree. At Mercury Bay in the Coromandel, a giant kauri with a diameter of over seven metres was estimated in 1889 to be more than 4000 years old by the botanist Thomas Kirk. But when another botanist, Thomas Cheeseman, counted the growth rings on its stump in 1914, these yielded the more conservative age of 1396 years. Then again, radiocarbon dating of the stump of Kopi (in Omahuta Forest, north of the Hokianga Harbour), which blew over in 1973, did give an age of about 4000 years.

TEN LARGEST KNOWN LIVING KAURI
(by volume)

Name	Volume (m^3)	Girth (m)	Trunk height (m)	Total height (m)	Location
1. Tane Mahuta*	244.5	13.77	17.68	51.5	Waipoua
2. Te Matua Ngahere*†	208.1	16.41	10.21	29.9	Waipoua
3. McGregor Kauri	170.6	13.69	12.25	40.8	Waipoua
4. Te Tangi o te Tui	155.1	12.38	13.10	50.9	Puketi
5. Moetangi No 1 (Ward kauri)	149.0	11.21	20.03	49.0	Warawara
6. Tanenui	135.7	10.08	18.29	47.2	Manaia
7. Yakas kauri*	134.2	12.29	12.04	43.9	Waipoua
8. Hokianga kauri	131.1	9.58	20.73	53.3	Omahuta
9. Tairua kauri	128.3	9.78	22.86	49.7	Coromandel
10. Moetangi No 1	118.5	10.62	11.44	not known	Warawara

* Most accessible to visitors
† Another kauri rediscovered in Waipoua Forest may be larger than Te Matua Ngahere
(Halkett and Sale 1986)

MEASURING UP

Dimensions of the largest kauri known and General Sherman, the giant sequoia

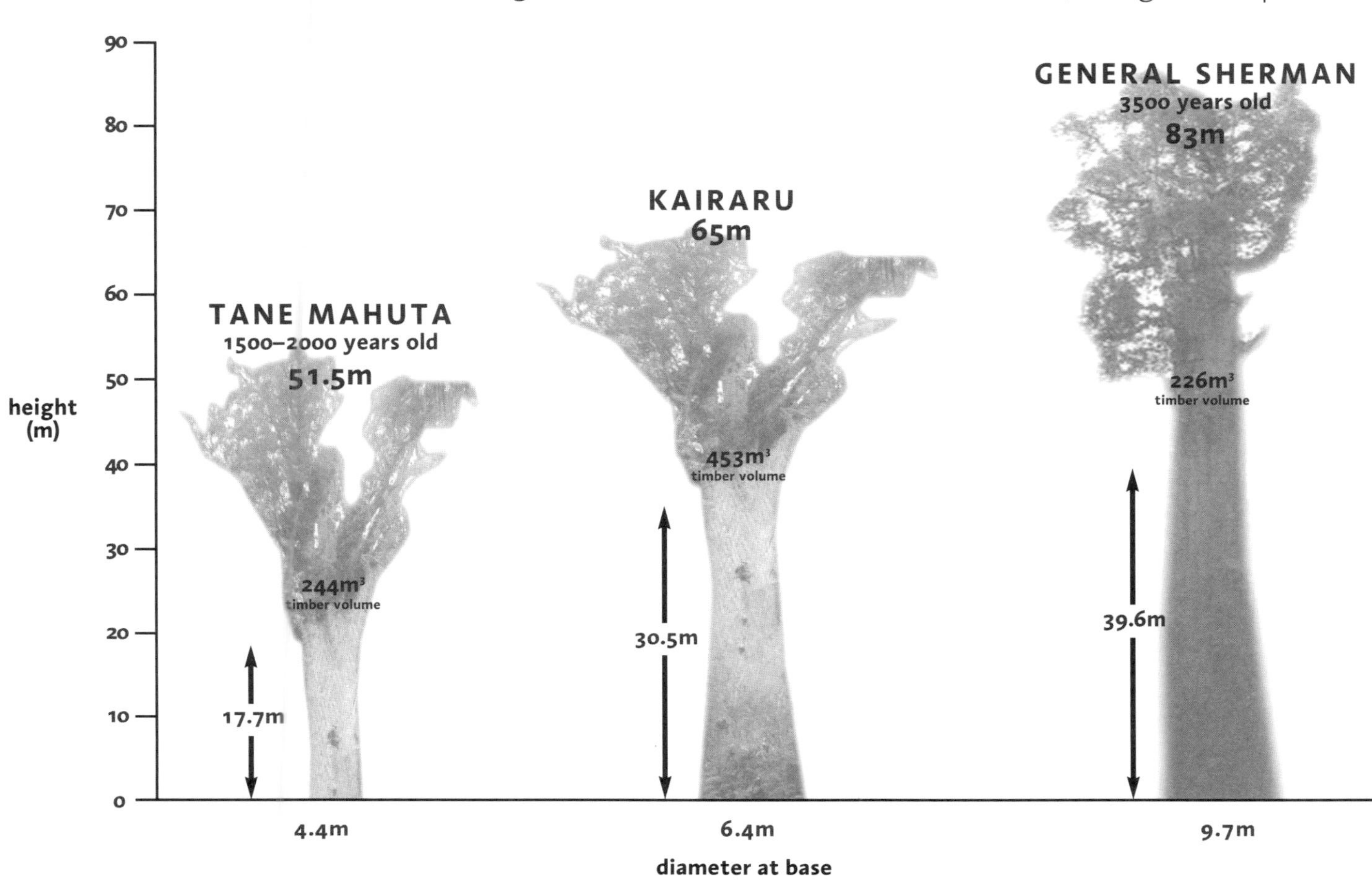

Rei Hamon's depiction of Nga Ariki brings the remaining largest kauri trees together in one bush scene dominated by their serene majesty.

Growth rates based on tree-ring cores from large samples of younger living trees confirm that age and size are not closely related, even on the same site. Age can vary by as much as 300 years for trees of the same diameter. So the largest kauri on any site may not necessarily be the oldest. By calculating the average growth rates for each stage of the tree's life cycle, it can be estimated that, in general, mature kauri will reach about 1.3 metres in diameter, which would give an average age of 600–700 years. Fewer trees reach two metres in diameter, giving an average age of about 1100 years. Trees of more than three metres diameter (equivalent to about 1700 years) are now extremely rare.

Growth rings can provide estimates only for the age of giant trees. No tree-coring instrument is large enough to penetrate to the heart of the largest living trees, and old trees are mostly hollow. Perhaps we should simply be satisfied to know that such trees are at least 1500 years old — it has never been polite to ask the age of revered elder statesmen. Although there is no reliable evidence that any living trees are more than 2000 years old, it would not be an extravagant claim for those trees long gone that exceeded the dimensions of Tane Mahuta (over four metres in diameter) or Te Matua Ngahere (over five metres in diameter).

Body building

As a conifer, kauri are not world record-holders in height, girth, or age, but they take their place as champion when it comes to producing high-quality straight-grained heart timber. The enormous yield of usable timber from mature kauri trees was of course to prove their downfall. The potential timber yield from Tane Mahuta, for instance, has been estimated as 244.5 cubic metres — enough to build at least ten modern houses. Even an 'average' mature kauri produces enough timber for a modest house. Such high yields can be attributed to the kauri's architecture or growth form.

The trunks of most giant conifers taper from base to tip, and are often supported by spreading buttresses at the base. Mature kauri, by contrast, are barrel-chested, and maintain a uniform girth from base to first branch. Their girth even increases at that point, as the massive lower branches are themselves over a metre in diameter where they leave the trunk. A whorl of branches all grow upwards at a similar acute angle to the trunk, much like supporting upturned spokes for the open umbrella formed by the crown.

Left The massive columns of these mature kauri in Waipoua Forest reveal the characteristic even girth from base to first branch that contributes to kauri being the world's top yielder of usable timber.

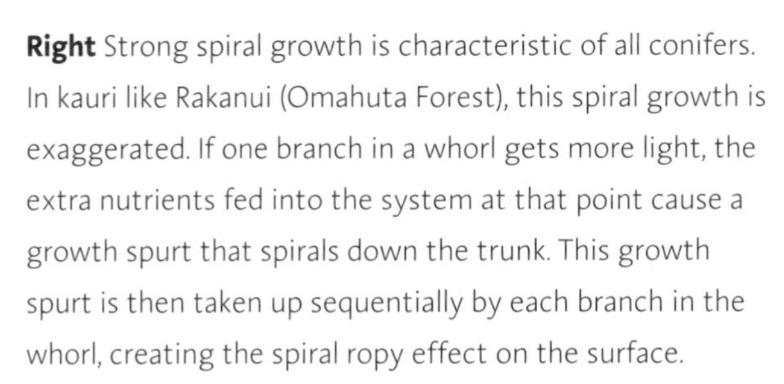

Right Strong spiral growth is characteristic of all conifers. In kauri like Rakanui (Omahuta Forest), this spiral growth is exaggerated. If one branch in a whorl gets more light, the extra nutrients fed into the system at that point cause a growth spurt that spirals down the trunk. This growth spurt is then taken up sequentially by each branch in the whorl, creating the spiral ropy effect on the surface.

This roadside scene in Waipoua Forest shows the changing form of kauri as it grows from seedling to ancient tree. Behind the foreground seedling on the left are several adolescent trees still retaining whorls of short branches. On the right, behind the group of kauri seedlings, a maturing 'ricker' has shed its lower branches. The large kauri in the background have the stout trunks and 'umbrella spoke' branches characteristic of mature trees.

Unlike mature kauri, adolescent trees have the more typical form of other conifers — a slender tapering trunk with whorls of short branches and a narrow triangular crown. As kauri reach thirty to fifty years of age, they begin to shed their lower branches and continue to do so until they emerge above the canopy of the forest. This shedding of branches below the crown results in the knot-free timber for which kauri is renowned. Trees in this stage of growth became known as 'rickers', after the name given to the naval masts and spars for which kauri were used in the earliest days of European exploration and exploitation.

Once a tree breaks through the forest canopy and sees the light, it leaves its adolescence behind. 'Growing up' gives way to 'growing out' as the tree settles into the serious adult business of building up wood and increasing its girth. This process of 'bulk-building' continues until the mature tree achieves its vast symmetrical column, a process that takes hundreds of years.

Achilles heels

The huge crown of the mature tree is balanced below ground by spreading lateral roots. Although these extend for large distances, kauri's main anchors are vertical 'peg' roots that descend up to five metres from the laterals. These peg roots can die if the subsoil is poorly drained. When this happens, kauri can become top-heavy and vulnerable to toppling by gale-force winds. Whole tracts of forest have been flattened in this way in the past (see page 50).

Equally vulnerable is kauri's dense mat of fine feeding roots, which extends from the lateral roots into the litter (shed bark, branchlets with leaves, cones and resin) that accumulates at the base of the tree. Over the years, trampling of this surface mat has lowered the life expectancy of the most-visited giant trees. Stephen King, co-founder of the Waipoua Forest Trust, says that Tane Mahuta has lost about thirty percent of its feeding root zone because of trampling — the reason for extending the fenced-off area around Waipoua's big trees. To compensate for the loss, in 2000 Te Roroa and the Waipoua Forest Trust spread a truckload of kauri litter around the giant tree's base. Tane Mahuta's feeding roots are already growing into this, and its crown is showing renewed vigour.

If sensitive toes were not enough, kauri roots also seem prone to fungi-induced foot rot, a problem that may have increased with the disturbance caused by human activities such as logging and roading. Foot rot may be the cause of death after such disturbance. In Trounson Kauri Park (just south of Waipoua Forest), dead kauri line the route of an old track, and according to John Beachman, Area Manager for the Department of Conservation, trees are still dying along the road through Waipoua Forest itself, even though the main impact was over seventy years ago. Stephen King tells of one mature tree on the Waipoua road that is now slowly dying after water was inadvertently deflected onto its root system during repairs to slip damage. Although this was remedied within three months, it was already too late to reverse the damage to the tree roots.

Strategies for a long life

No one has come up with a conclusive explanation for the outstanding success of the few ancient kauri — nor for any of the world's other truly majestic ancient trees. Location, chance, slow growth rates, effective defence mechanisms, and genetics probably all contribute.

Perhaps the largest kauri individuals grew on 'prime real estate', where soil, moisture, light, and temperature provided the best possible conditions. But many of the giant kauri still living in Waipoua Forest occupy swampy sites and infertile soils. Others grow on the steep dry slopes or ridges where more 'ordinary' kauri are now concentrated. These sites may of course merely reflect chance survival in areas that were inaccessible during the logging years or had unsuitable soils for agriculture.

Even more remarkable than the escape of some large kauri from logging and land clearance is their survival through more than 1000 years of catastrophic natural disturbances. Gales, landslides, fires, and floods devastate the New Zealand landscape often enough for modern ecologists to recognise natural disturbance as a major influence in the patterns and processes that shape the vegetation. When the effects of human disturbance are added to the mix, the conditions present today under any 1000-year-old kauri are unlikely to bear much resemblance to the conditions that set the young seedling on its way to such a long life.

Outliving the competition is a recognised strategy that enables slow-growing conifers to hold their own against faster-growing trees. But as a tree survives into maturity, its life span will depend on how effectively it wards off damage and decay. As the centre of an aging tree becomes inactive, the risk of insect attack and decay increases. To counteract this risk, some long-lived conifers produce resin.

Resin or gum oozes from the bark, leaves, and cones of all kauri trees, and large amounts form where branches fork. At first glance, such copious 'bleeding' might seem life-threatening and of limited biological advantage. Indeed, the practice well into the twentieth century of bleeding kauri to extract gum damaged many of the large trees and shortened their lives. The tree's high resin content also increases its susceptibility to fire — and deliberate fires contributed to the loss of kauri forests in the nineteenth and early twentieth centuries. But the interference of people aside, natural exudation of resin seals any damaged surfaces, the soft protective layer hardening on exposure to light and air. Producing resin therefore slows the onset of rot and contributes to the continuing health and vigour of even ancient hollow trees like Tane Mahuta and Te Matua Ngahere.

Excluding the competition is also an effective survival strategy. Kauri excels at patch protection. The litter that accumulates under kauri trees contains mostly decay-resistant woody material such as branches, bark, and cones. The huge quantity of nutrients that accumulates in the metre-high mounds that build up under mature trees is inaccessible to most other plants. Kauri itself, with the help of specialist bacteria and fungi, is extremely efficient in its use of the nutrients stored in its own litter. Indirect measurements of tree bulk-building (based on the nitrogen content of litter) give efficiency values for kauri forest that are almost twice those of other forests. Kauri is the ultimate recycler.

Over the life of the forest, the highly acidic tannin-rich material contained in kauri litter leaches the nutrients out of the underlying soil. Under long-lived kauri, this nutrient leaching eventually induces a depleted acidic soil known as an 'egg-cup podzol'. When this coincides with poor drainage, an impervious iron pan (a hard layer in the subsoil) can develop. Both egg-cup podzols and iron pans persist in the landscape as legacies of kauri long after the kauri forest itself has disappeared. Not only have the kauri's forest competitors been excluded — in some places where such soils are extensive, such as the Ahipara plateau south of Ninety Mile Beach, only stunted heath vegetation can now survive.

Many of the world's giant old trees have lineages that stretch far back into the geologic past, as fossil records show. Within such royal bloodlines, genetic superiority probably plays a significant part in the success of these long-living trees. On this assumption, seed from Tane Mahuta is being used to propagate seedlings for the Millennium Kauri Project. This joint venture between local Te Roroa Maori and the Waipoua Forest Trust aims to restore kauri forest on farmland next to Waipoua Forest.

An ancient lineage

The kauri is a living link with New Zealand's most distant past. On a scale that spans geologic time and the Southern Hemisphere, kauri forests have survived major shifts in the continental plates and the splitting up of the ancient continent of Gondwana. The gradual isolation of New Zealand from its neighbours took place after they had developed a shared flora and pre-mammalian fauna. New Zealand's unique plants and animals then evolved from these ancient ancestors.

Kauri belongs to one of the oldest existing conifer families, Araucariaceae, which has a fossil record stretching back about 200 million years to the age of the dinosaurs. Today, this family is found only in the Southern Hemisphere, although it extended across the Equator into the Northern Hemisphere until about 135 million years ago. As for most cone-bearing families (gymnosperms), the geographic area occupied by Araucariaceae began shrinking dramatically about 30–40 million years ago as the more sophisticated flowering plants (angiosperms) proliferated to become the most dominant plants world-wide.

Kauri ancestors seem to have evolved in the Australia–New Zealand region about 135 million years ago, when the two countries were still close together as part of Gondwana. Recognisable kauri-type pollen appears in New Zealand 70 million years ago. New Zealand kauri itself possibly appeared 20 million years ago, and was widespread by 7 million years ago — kauri-type pollen was then present as far south as Invercargill. During the same time, other recognisable New Zealand conifer ancestors appeared, as did the forebears of creatures unique to New Zealand such as tuatara, moa, and kiwi.

Until recently, only two genera, *Agathis* (kauri and its close cousins) and *Araucaria* (trees like Norfolk pine and monkey-puzzle), were thought to have survived from this once diverse family, with most species now being found in the tropics. But in 1994, Australian botanists announced the exciting discovery of a third new genus with one living species — the Wollemi pine. Intermediate in character between the other two genera, the Wollemi pine is a true relict. Only forty trees still exist in the wild, hidden in a steep and narrow gorge somewhere on the Central Tablelands of New South Wales. Growing only a few hundred kilometres from Australia's biggest city, this botanical missing link has to be the find of the century.

Patches, patterns, and processes

Before the arrival of people, much of Northland, Auckland, and the Coromandel Peninsula was covered in forest. Interrupted only by areas of wetland or scrub-covered terrain recovering from natural disturbances, forest extended from the coast to the tops of the mountain ranges. Much of the forest below 600 metres altitude contained kauri. Lowland areas recovering from natural disturbance often contained stumps and logs of kauri or egg-cup podzols — evidence that kauri forests had once been present.

Today, only about five percent of the pre-human kauri forest is left, and this is scattered across the landscape in isolated patches. Kauri now generally occupies sites with poor soils on spurs, ridges, and plateaus, often in steep and broken terrain. Most forests that still contain kauri are restricted to areas that were of little use to settlers bent on extracting the most accessible timber and clearing the most productive land for farming. Historical human disturbance therefore contributes to the pattern of today's forest patches. Such patches are unlikely to be representative of the original forests, and Peter Bellingham, forest ecologist and kauri enthusiast, points out that it is difficult if not impossible to know what these forests were really like. Ecologists can make a better fist of interpreting the dynamic processes that formed and renewed them, as similar processes still operate today.

Opposite above A typical group or stand of mature kauri clustered on a ridge in the Manaia Forest Sanctuary, Coromandel, carry their crowns high above the forest canopy formed by broad-leaved trees and tree ferns.

Opposite below In many previously logged areas, dense stands of kauri rickers are now vigorously regenerating on spurs and ridges, initiating the mosaic pattern typical of kauri forest. Here, kauri is re-establishing in the scrub of Kaitoke Valley, Great Barrier Island.

Community and companions

Despite their remnant nature, these northern forests are still the most diverse and structurally complex in New Zealand. They often contain some twenty different tree species per hectare, and have many of the characteristic plant families and life forms of subtropical forests — trees with buttressed trunks, tree ferns, nikau palms, festoons of lianes, orchids, and perching plants. Many of the trees and shrubs that grow with kauri, such as kohekohe, taraire, maire tawake, and mangaeo, are the only New Zealand representatives of common tropical Pacific genera. Kauri itself has twelve close cousins plus two subspecies that all grow in the subtropical and tropical regions of Australia and the Pacific — five of them on New Caledonia, an island the size of Northland (see map below). New Zealand kauri, the most southern species, is found only in New Zealand and only as far south as a rough line that extends from Kawhia Harbour in the west to Katikati and the Kaimai Range in the east. The forests that make up this northern subtropical element of the New Zealand flora are also found only this far south (see map opposite).

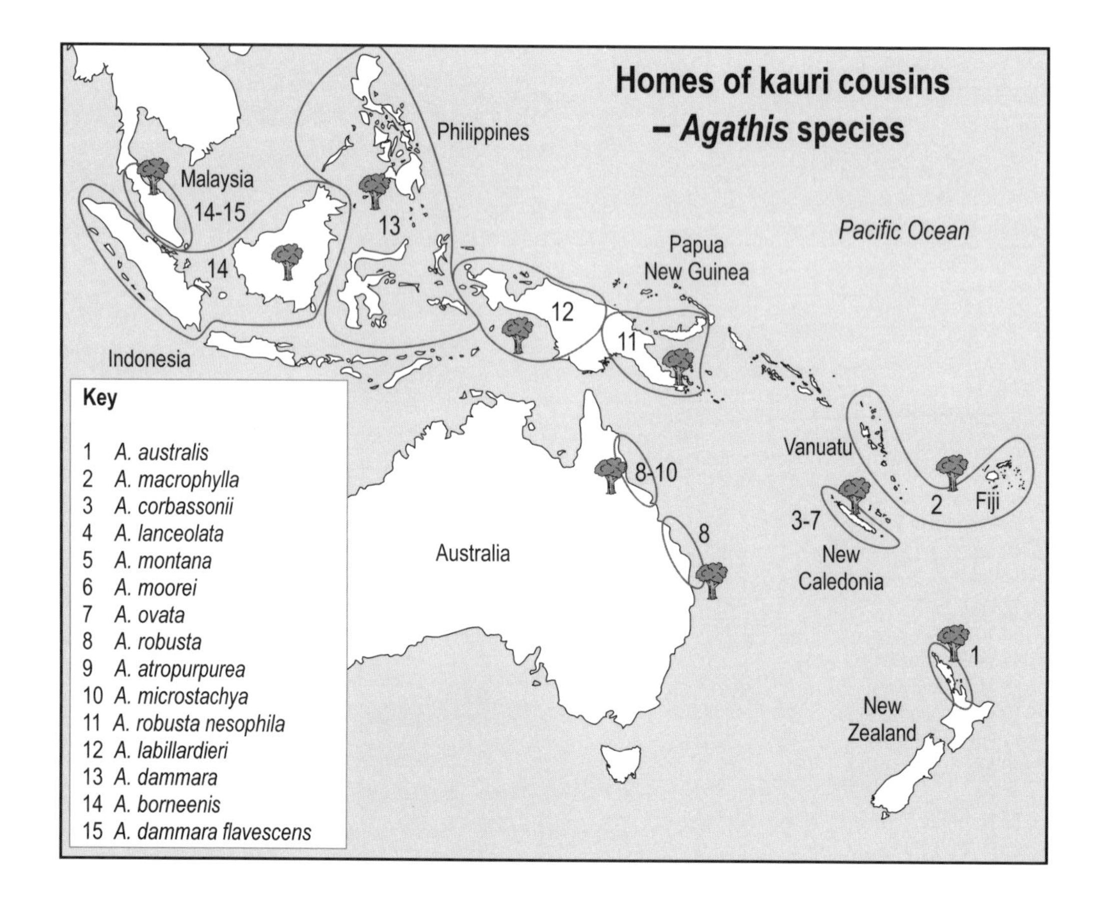

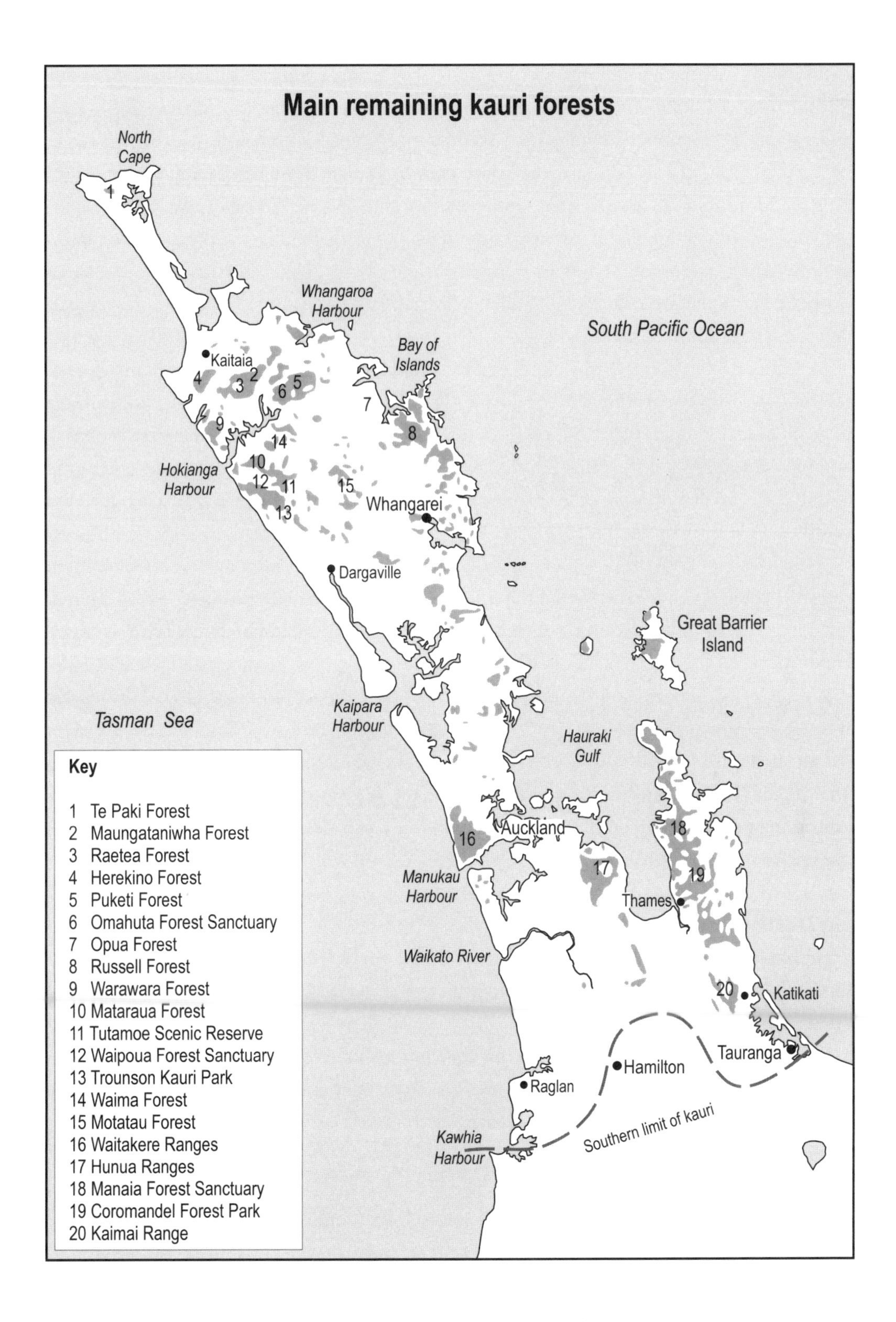
Main remaining kauri forests
North Cape
Whangaroa Harbour
South Pacific Ocean
Bay of Islands
Kaitaia
Hokianga Harbour
Whangarei
Dargaville
Great Barrier Island
Tasman Sea
Kaipara Harbour
Hauraki Gulf
Auckland
Manukau Harbour
Thames
Waikato River
Katikati
Tauranga
Hamilton
Raglan
Kawhia Harbour
Southern limit of kauri
Key
1 Te Paki Forest
2 Maungataniwha Forest
3 Raetea Forest
4 Herekino Forest
5 Puketi Forest
6 Omahuta Forest Sanctuary
7 Opua Forest
8 Russell Forest
9 Warawara Forest
10 Mataraua Forest
11 Tutamoe Scenic Reserve
12 Waipoua Forest Sanctuary
13 Trounson Kauri Park
14 Waima Forest
15 Motatau Forest
16 Waitakere Ranges
17 Hunua Ranges
18 Manaia Forest Sanctuary
19 Coromandel Forest Park
20 Kaimai Range

'Typical' mature kauri forest contains groups of large kauri that emerge above the forest canopy of other conifers and shade-tolerant northern broad-leaved trees like taraire and towai. In the most diverse mature stands, up to nine other conifers (of which rimu, miro, and mountain totara are the most common) can grow with kauri. In western Northland, mountain totara often co-dominates with kauri. In young stands, the light-demanding conifer, tanekaha, often co-dominates, but is generally out-competed by kauri as the stands age. Such stands are common in eastern Northland. In more southern districts, particularly on the Coromandel Peninsula and the Kaimai Range, kauri trees co-dominate with hard beech.

A rich variety of small trees and shrubs, many of which grow only in kauri forest, thrives in the lower open tiers of the forest. 'Kauri grass', a tall sedge, and the scrambling liane, kiekie, dominate the dense tall ground cover. Only a few low-growing herbs, ferns, and mosses establish in the thick litter. Many kauri companions have restricted ranges even within the northern region — the extreme example being Bartlett's rata, which is not found south of Te Hapua on the Parengarenga Harbour in the Far North.

Not much is known about the complex community-level ecology of these northern forests. Ecologists have now shown that distributions of dominant tree species at Waipoua, including kauri, reflect altitude and topography, which underlie much of the varied composition of this forest. Peter Bellingham suggests that both chance establishment from randomly available seed sources (a direct result of the fragmented nature of the remaining forests) and time since the last disturbance also contribute to differences in composition. Many species associated with kauri appear only at certain stages as a new stand develops after disturbance. Some orchids and understorey shrubs grow where young kauri is establishing in manuka communities, some only in kauri ricker stands, and others only in mature kauri forests.

Dynamics and disturbance

To a large extent, the distribution patterns of all species in the northern forests reflect landscape disturbances on various ecological and geological time scales as much as they reflect relationships and habitat needs.

On an ecological time scale, it seems that mature kauri stands have always formed a mosaic of patches across the landscape, much as they do now. As early as 1859, when many of the original forests were still intact, the Austrian geologist Ferdinand von Hochstetter described this pattern:

> *These kauri groups vary greatly in extent. They often occupy several square miles; sometimes there are only thirty or forty trees clustered together. . . . Closely*

> *connected with this peculiarity . . . is the other, that the trees of one and the same group or grove are usually of nearly the same age. . . . In these clumps the kauri tree suffers no forest tree by its side; only smaller trees and shrubs compose the undergrowth.*
>
> (HALKETT AND SALE 1986)

The similar age of trees in such mature kauri groups or patches is highlighted by the apparent absence of regenerating seedlings and young saplings in the shade under their dense canopies. This absence or gap in the kauri's age structure in mature stands contrasts with the ability of kauri seedlings to establish and grow vigorously under the more open manuka and kanuka scrubland that sprang up in areas devastated by logging or burning.

Early botanists like Leonard Cockayne, who worked with the Lands Department in the early twentieth century, interpreted this dynamic process as an indication that kauri was a light-demanding species that would ultimately be replaced in the mature forest by shade-tolerant broad-leaved trees. Others saw this process of replacement as cyclical, with patches dominated by kauri swapping places with those dominated by other conifers and broad-leaved trees in a process that moved across the landscape in space and time to create the observed mosaic. Later scientists suggested that larger-scale dynamics were operating. Since native conifer forests elsewhere in New Zealand also revealed apparent gaps in their age structure, they argued that recent climatic change was shifting the balance in favour of broad-leaved species. Conifers were on their way out.

In the last decade or so, botanists have now recognised that many such 'regeneration gaps' can be explained by the responses of conifers like kauri to disturbance on different scales. By examining kauri dynamics over a time scale of several thousand years, ecologist John Ogden has come up with an elegant concept that accommodates most of the earlier interpretations.

In this concept, a cycle of replacement is triggered by any major disturbance that flattens the existing forest. A dense same-aged group or 'cohort' of kauri will establish through the manuka and kanuka that first occupy the bare site. Any gaps created by natural thinning in this dense stand will be taken up by the expanding crowns of adjacent kauri. This prevents light-demanding kauri seedlings from gaining a foothold. The seedlings are unable to establish until some of the mature kauri trees fall to create larger gaps, after maybe 300–400 years. A whole crop of kauri seedlings can then establish in these gaps to produce a new cohort. This new cohort then has to compete with faster-growing broad-leaved trees to fill the gaps. It will therefore be less dense, smaller, and less even-aged than the first cohort. Even so, its establishment will maintain kauri on the site for a further 600–1000 years. On some sites, a third smaller and even less coherent cohort may develop in the same way.

At any stage, the whole cycle can be interrupted and restarted by smaller-scale disturbances such as gales or erosion, further complicating the landscape mosaic. Disturbances of this kind can be more frequent on the ridge-top sites 'favoured' by kauri, so there are more frequent opportunities for kauri seedlings to establish on these sites. This may better explain the presence of dense multi-aged kauri on ridge tops, rather than kauri's supposed preference for dry sites with low fertility. On other sites, only a few kauri need survive to ensure that seedlings of this long-lived species can take advantage of any major disturbance and start the cycle again.

Today, the area of young kauri stands regenerating in this way far exceeds that of the remnant original forests. In many kauri areas logged and burnt during the nineteenth and early twentieth centuries, then later abandoned after the failure of farming on kauri-depleted soils, kauri is busy demonstrating its age-old ability to benefit from major disturbance. Many scrub-covered spurs and ridges in Northland, on Great Barrier Island, and on the Coromandel are now resurgent with vigorously regenerating kauri. Despite the concern of early conservationists in the 1940s and 1950s such as Professor W. R. McGregor of the University of Auckland (see Chapter 9, On the turn), kauri is indeed proving itself the ultimate survivor.

Understanding the dynamics of any forest system in New Zealand is complicated by the added impact of introduced browsing animals (see Chapter 10, Sinister forces). Although the forests once contained fauna that focused on plants for fodder — for example, the moa that became extinct after Maori ancestors migrated here — the degree to which the flora became adapted to browsing is still being energetically debated. Regardless, the introduction of deer, goats, pigs, and possums had repercussions that saw scientists making scapegoats of them all to account for any perceived deterioration in the native forests. Only in the last decade or so, as the major role of landscape disturbance became recognised, have introduced animals been seen as just one of the many interacting factors that dictate pattern and process in New Zealand's forests.

Beating a retreat

Although stands of young kauri are regenerating vigorously in many places, kauri shows no sign of spreading naturally beyond its present restricted northern distribution. Yet planted kauri are capable of growing in much colder climates as far south as Stewart Island. Forest ecologist Rob Allen reports that natural seedlings have now been discovered establishing beyond stands of planted kauri in North Canterbury, 1000 kilometres south of the species' present natural limit. Understanding why kauri and many of its associated species are restricted to the northern region involves a journey back through the last few million years to look at distribution patterns on a geological time scale. During this period, tectonic disturbances that included sea-level changes, mountain-building episodes, glaciation, and volcanic eruptions shaped the major vegetation patterns still recognisable today.

Much of what is known about these vegetation and climate patterns is gleaned from fossil pollen records and sub-fossil wood preserved in peat bogs and swamps. Like other native conifers, kauri reached its greatest latitudinal extent about 30–40 million years ago. Rising sea levels about five million years ago and the progressive destruction of old leached soils by volcanic eruptions and periods of glaciation during the last two million years saw kauri retreating steadily northwards. This retreat continued until kauri was eventually confined to the northern region.

The northern region retained its forests throughout these two million years. But the presence and abundance of kauri fluctuated during the alternating warm and cold climates that accompanied the periods of glaciation. Several layers of ancient kauri logs and stumps lie preserved in the extensive peat bogs and swamps of the north. Radiocarbon dates have revealed that the oldest logs are aged at least 45,000 years (the limit of radiocarbon dating). Log layers dated at different places give ages grouped around 35,000 years, 10,000–5000 years, and 5000–2000 years. Some of the forests represented by these layers seem to have died as the result of catastrophic climatic and landscape-scale disturbances that accompanied the glacial periods. Others seem to have collapsed more gradually as areas of bog developed.

In some areas of the northernmost Aupouri Peninsula, sub-fossil logs lie toppled in all directions, many of them charred. Their death may have been the result of fires in peat that dried out during the droughts accompanying advances of the ice. In other areas, the logs are aligned, suggesting wind-throw by hurricane-strength storms. Influxes of the sea caused by tsunamis may also have triggered the death of ancient kauri forests in low-lying areas like the Kaimaumau Swamp and Lake Ohia near Doubtless Bay in the Far North.

Kauri seems to have been sparse during both the final advance of the ice 25,000 years ago and the warming that began 10,000 years ago. Only about 7000 years ago did suitable climatic conditions allow kauri to begin spreading southwards once more, probably expanding outwards from small 'refuge' areas throughout much of its present range. It had reached its present boundary by about 3000 years ago. South of this boundary, it was probably the more fertile young soils derived from volcanic activity, rather than climatic factors, that continued to exclude kauri in favour of other more competitive conifers and broad-leaved trees. North of the boundary, some of the kauri forests destroyed by large-scale disturbances were unable to re-establish on the waterlogged or acidic podzol soils left by their forebears.

With the arrival of people about 1000 years ago, New Zealand's forests faced a new major geographic-scale disturbance that was to change the landscape dramatically. The onset of widespread human-induced forest destruction about 700 years ago, and the eventual conversion of forest cover to pasture, meant that any potential for kauri forests to spread further south naturally was lost.

TIME CAPSULES

Climatic history is being gleaned from both living and swamp-preserved kauri. John Ogden and a team of dendrochronologists based at the University of Auckland have now established cross-matched tree-ring chronologies based on hundreds of living kauri that accurately date back for about 1000 years. These chronologies agree for trees as far apart as Kaitaia and the Bay of Plenty. The team hope to extend their chronologies back 5000 years by linking them with tree-ring chronologies of about 3000 years for wood excavated from swamps. Such chronologies have now been cross-matched for swamp kauri from Dargaville and the Waikato, indicating the existence of ancient region-wide patterns.

Living-tree chronologies show strong correlations with El Nino weather patterns, and John Ogden thinks the patterns should be equally clear in the swamp kauri. His sights are now set on developing similarly accurate chronologies from 45,000-year-old swamp kauri trees:

> *We won't be able to extend an accurate cross-matched chronology back for 45,000 years in my lifetime, but what we will be able to do is develop accurately dated 500-year chronologies that fall somewhere about that time period. Even if we don't know the exact starting date for that set of years, the patterns can still tell us a lot about past climate.*

By recreating the climates of the past, kauri researchers will then be able to help predict the climates of the future.

Gretel Boswijk, a member of the dendrochronology team based at the University of Auckland, examines a disc cut from a large kauri log excavated from a swamp near Dargaville and taken to Nelson's Kaihu Kauri for milling. Tree rings counted on this disc will contribute to cross-matched chronologies spanning more than 2000 years.

Chapter 3

The first spar seekers

Early European and Maori contacts, 1769–1809

Strangers from the sea

Signal fires smoke all along the coast. Canoes set out to sea, their crews armed and ready for action. At Te Whanganui-o-Hei (Mercury Bay, Coromandel), the people have been under attack for some time and are well prepared. But it is not a war canoe they boldly set out to challenge on a November evening in 1769. It is a floating island or giant bird, peopled by strange beings. White-skinned and strangely clad, these beings speak an unknown tongue and behave inexplicably in response to the ritual challenges. The Mercury Bay people are encountering Captain James Cook on his first circumnavigation of the New Zealand coastline. This and similar meetings with strangers from the sea in the late eighteenth century changed the Maori world for ever, particularly in the north.

Grand ideas lay behind these late-eighteenth-century European voyages to the South Pacific — the search for El Dorado, the quest for the elusive southern continent, and the growth of scientific exploration. The voyages were also the expression of intensifying competition

The contrasting worlds of Maori inhabitants and European explorers are reflected in Sydney Parkinson's engraving of Te Puta o te Paretauhinu pa at Mercury Bay on Cook's first voyage in 1768–1771. The rock arch has since collapsed.

between the English and the French for naval supremacy, access to wealth, and expansion of Empire. A specific and pressing incentive was the search for new timber resources to rebuild navies depleted by years of warfare.

It was not the learned Royal Society scientists on board Cook's *Endeavour* who noted the presence of one of the world's best timber trees in Mercury Bay. In their forays ashore to collect plant specimens, these scientists somehow overlooked the kauri towering above the skyline forests. It was instead the officers of an entrepreneurial French expedition led by Marc-Joseph Marion du Fresne, searching in the Bay of Islands in 1772 for suitable timber to replace broken spars, who first described the conspicuous and handsome tree:

. . . the tree which prevails most in all the forests is the olive-leaved cedar. I had cedars of this variety cut down whose trunks were more than a hundred feet long, from the ground to the lowest branches, and fifty-two inches in diameter. The trees are very resinous; the resin is white and transparent, and gives out an agreeable smell like incense when burnt. It appeared to me that this cedar is the commonest and highest tree in the country; its wood is elastic, and I judged it very suitable for making ship's masts.

(HALKETT AND SALE 1986, FROM THE JOURNAL OF CROZET, SECOND IN COMMAND ON THE *Mascarin*)

Although the French were eventually to sail away empty-handed, their attempt to extract kauri for spars was to be the first of many. Their expedition proved the most disastrous of the early encounters between Europeans and Maori, despite a promising beginning.

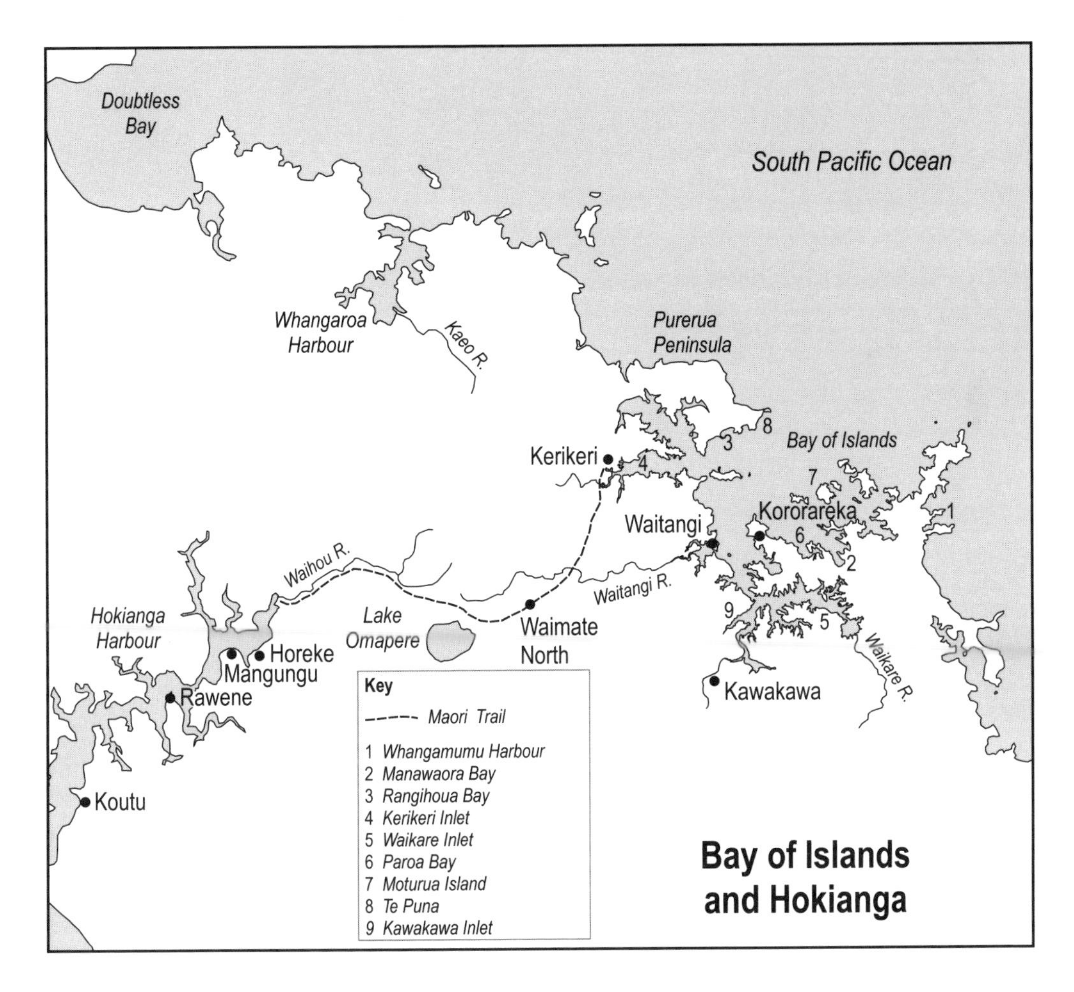

Contact, confusion, and conflict

Before Marion du Fresne's two ships, the *Mascarin* and the *Marquis de Castries*, arrived in the Bay of Islands (barely three years after Cook's visit in 1769) there had been another visitation — by the Frenchman Jean-François-Marie de Surville in December 1769 on the *St Jean Baptiste*. Soon realising that these strangers from the sea were human like themselves, northern Maori treated them accordingly. The occupants of the ships were greeted with the challenges and courtesies extended to all visitors, and generous quantities of food and other gifts were offered. Such hospitality was an expression of wealth and chiefly mana (ancestral status maintained by proven prowess). Part of a reciprocal system of exchange, it carried the expectation of similar generosity in return.

For their part, the voyagers were accustomed to replenishing their stores on foreign shores as cheaply as possible, either by barter with 'savages' in return for European trifles, or more simply by plunder of apparently unowned or abandoned resources. Friendly intentions on both sides were not enough to counteract the misunderstandings induced by such different views of what 'behove a gentleman'. Although most encounters were amicable, Cook's men sometimes responded to canoes laden with aggressively chanting warriors or to the occasional seizing of goods by shooting the perpetrators. Despite being received with generous hospitality by the people at Tokerau (Doubtless Bay), Surville reacted swiftly to perceived hostility, burning canoes and villages and taking a chief captive. In the Maori view, any such insult or injury required retaliation before the all-important lost mana and associated community well-being could be restored. Retaliation (utu) was the reverse side of the coin of reciprocity. Maori expectations of equality and reciprocity were constantly being set against European assumptions of superiority — opposing world views that inevitably distorted and directed their encounters.

It was against this background that the well-meaning Marion du Fresne and his masting party arrived in the Bay of Islands on 4 May 1772.

Masts and massacres

For more than a month, from early May to early June 1772, the *Mascarin* and the *Marquis de Castries* lay peacefully at anchor in the Bay of Islands. Marion du Fresne's men established camps ashore and enjoyed growing friendships with the local inhabitants:

> *. . . the savages were always among us at our settlements and on board our vessels, and in exchange for nails they furnished us with fish, quail, wood pigeons and wild duck; they ate with our sailors and helped them in their labours. . . . Our young men, attracted by the winning ways of the savages, and by the friendliness of their daughters, overran the villages every day, even making*

journeys inland to hunt the ducks, and taking with them the savages, who carried them across marshes and rivers as easily as a man would carry a child.

(Ollivier 1985, from the journal of Crozet, second-in-command on the *Mascarin*)

Paradise indeed; Marion du Fresne, a devotee of Rousseau's philosophy of the noble savage, was in his element.

The French needed timber to replace the twenty-metre foremast and fourteen-metre bowsprit of the *Marquis de Castries*, damaged earlier in a collision between the two ships. They were taken by Maori guides five kilometres (roughly equivalent to the French 'league') inland from Manawaora to a stand of tall kauri rickers. Although the terrain was both hilly and beset by swamps waist-deep in water, Marion du Fresne had a masting camp set up here. Another camp was established behind the beach for the workmen.

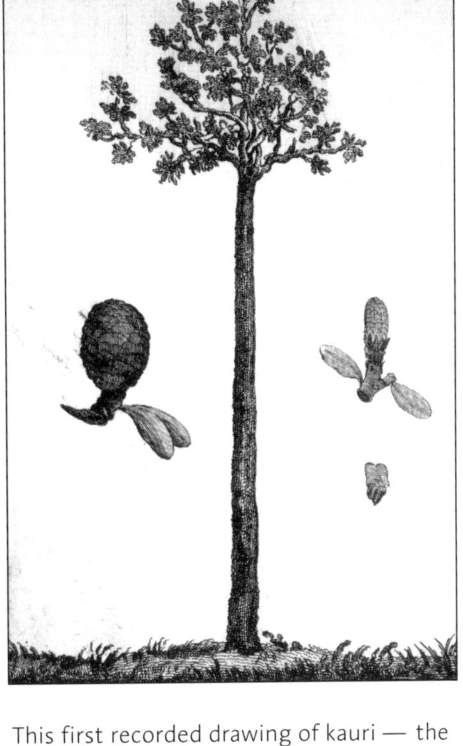

This first recorded drawing of kauri — the 'olive-leaved cedar' — with its male and female cones came from Marion du Fresne's ill-fated expedition to the Bay of Islands in 1772.

On the 29th May, we began to cut the bowsprit, which, although the most accessible [tree], was growing in a precipice, from which it had to be dragged out and, in the felling, prevented from slipping down the slope. Thus we took the necessary precautions for holding it by means of strong ropes. The equipment was set up for hauling it out of the ravine, which was a very difficult operation: finally after a lot of trouble we brought it up to the top of the mountain. . . . While this mast was being trimmed to an octagonal shape, we cut the foremast, which we took from further into the woods. These works employed two-thirds of our crews and heavy equipment was required to drag the pieces of timber along such a hilly path.

(Ollivier 1985, from the journal of Roux, Lieutenant on the *Mascarin*)

Groups of local people sometimes came to observe their progress. Although some occasionally helped to haul on the tackle falls, they were not regularly involved in this labour. As they participated fully in wooding and hunting expeditions, for which they were paid with desirable pieces of hoop-iron and nails, it is possible they viewed the masting operation with some ambivalence. As Toi Marsden explains, in the Maori world the felling of a kauri for making a canoe was a significant and infrequent event accompanied by long involved rituals and karakia. The French lack of ceremony and protocol must have seemed both inappropriate and inauspicious.

The French officers took it in turns to oversee the masting work, which left them plenty of leisure for hunting and exploring. Despite such pleasant preoccupations, they could not help but be aware of local comings and goings that included preparations for skirmishes. All the officers understood that many of the local chiefs they had befriended were at war. But what the French did not know was that these skirmishes were part of an ongoing shift in political dominance over the whole Bay of Islands area.

It seems likely that the attention lavished on Marion du Fresne was merely part of the vying for position and power among opposing tribal groups — patronage and 'possession' of the French being an enviable expression of mana. One of the chiefs from whom the French received such patronage was 'Tacoury' — Te Kauri (his name a nice irony). This man, who had a large fortified village east of Manawaora, was affiliated to various groups of Nga Puhi, at that time infiltrating into the area. The chiefs occupying the islands, including Moturua where the French were camped, seemed to have been affiliated to Ngati Pou and Ngati Uru, previous holders of the authority over the area. In favouring these chiefs, the French unwittingly became a threat to Te Kauri's perhaps still tenuous supremacy. In bestowing their favours unevenly, the French no doubt also unwittingly offended some chiefs. In flaunting their acquisitions, the favoured chiefs further fanned the flames of tribal unrest.

At the same time, the French had outstayed their welcome. They had placed extra and insatiable demands on local resources of fish, fowl, and firewood. They had souvenired carvings, canoes, and other treasured items — apparently without compunction. They had inevitably and repeatedly transgressed against local practice and protocol. The traditions recorded in the area suggest that the final straw came when Marion du Fresne against all protest fished from a particular beach near Manawaora:

> *There came a day when the foreigners rowed ashore in order to net fish on the beach at Manawaora. The Maori people scolded them for this, as the beach was tapu to some of Te Kauri's people (the people who lived at Whangamumu). Some people from there had been drowned in the Bay of Islands, and had been*

cast ashore on this beach. Although the people of Ngaati Pou told them angrily not to do this (for they were afraid that Te Kauri's people would attack them in order to obtain recompense for the violation of their tapu), the foreigners took no notice, and persisted in drawing their net on the beach. Then Ngaati Pou became very sad, and no longer visited the ships. . . . The foreigners [had] violated the tapu of Manawaora by netting fish there and eating those fish; it was this that made the desecration of the tapu such a grave offence.

(SALMOND 1991, FROM ORBELL)

Four days later, Te Kauri took inevitable and necessary action. Despite being explicitly warned of his intentions and despite growing signs of unrest and antagonism among the local people, Marion du Fresne was still naively convinced that 'since I do them nothing but good, surely they will not do me any harm'. He willingly accompanied Te Kauri on yet another fishing expedition — to the same beach. There, while they dragged in the fishing net together, he and his men from the *Mascarin* were bludgeoned to death by their Maori companions — an elegant if exacting act of utu. Then, to further avert the extreme spiritual harm done by their perceived cannibalism in eating fish under tapu (equivalent to eating the flesh of the drowned men), the French officers in turn became the victims of ritual cannibalism.

Acts of utu did not stop there. Next morning a party of seamen from the *Marquis de Castries* was ambushed and killed while collecting firewood. All the French camps came under increasing threat by other groups elated at Te Kauri's success. At the masting camps,

In this reconstruction, an unsuspecting and naive Marion du Fresne is about to be bludgeoned to death by Te Kauri's men in revenge for the French netting fish on a tapu beach at Manawaora.

Crozet reluctantly abandoned the kauri spars, now a hard-won two-thirds of the way to the beach. He achieved an orderly retreat from the inland camp, despite being surrounded by up to 1000 chanting warriors. Equally orderly, these warriors obeyed their chief's command to sit down behind a line the steel-nerved Crozet drew on the beach. It was not until the French launched their boats that the warriors at last launched their attack. It was not until then that Crozet opened fire.

The French musket fire left scores of warriors dead on the beach. Over the next few days, the French attacked Te Kauri's village on the mainland and Paeroa pa on Moturua, where warriors continued to threaten their camp. By the time the French had rescued their gear and successfully evacuated the camp, they had killed several hundred of the local inhabitants and burnt their villages. Over the next month, while the disillusioned French completed necessary repairs, loaded stores, and fashioned makeshift masts to replace the abandoned kauri spars, they continued to repel Maori attacks. Despite the courage displayed by various groups of local people, their canoes, palisades, flax cloaks, and stone or wooden weapons were useless against carronades and muskets.

The French at last sailed out of the Bay, feeling utterly betrayed by the transformation of friendship into fury. This first failure to obtain kauri for spars left behind expanding ripples of tribal retaliation and recrimination. Ngati Pou and Ngati Uru were in turn eventually forced out of the Bay of Islands for their own failure to prevent the French fishing transgression that had led to such disastrous consequences.

Convicts, colonies, and cargoes

If the late eighteenth century was a time of political turmoil in northern Maori New Zealand, it was even more so in Europe. The closing decades of the century saw wars of independence (America), civil revolution (France), and wars between nations (the Napoleonic wars). Expansion of the British navy took place alongside loss of access to American timber supplies. At the same time, the establishment of Pacific colonies was being suggested to accommodate the growing numbers of convicts that reflected new draconian laws against theft of property. Convicts could conveniently be punished by transportation to someone else's backyard.

James Matra and Sir Joseph Banks, participants in Cook's 1768–1771 expedition, argued for the attractions of New South Wales. The expense of transporting convicts such distances could be compensated by loading timber and flax (for cordage) from nearby New Zealand for the return trip. The proposal triggered the first extractions of timber for spars from the Hauraki Gulf, less than a decade after the establishment of the penal colony at Port Jackson (Sydney) in 1788.

Kahikatea to kauri

At least four significant ships called at Hauraki between 1794 and 1801 in search of spar cargoes. The first was the *Fancy*, a small brig commissioned by the East India Company for trade between India and the new colony at Port Jackson. Late in 1794, Dell and his crew felled 213 trees with cross-cut saws, then departed with a full cargo for Sydney, leaving the rest of the spars in the care of the local people for later collection. The *Fancy* was followed by the *Hunter* in 1798, loading spars for China that probably included those cut earlier by Dell. Finally two larger ships, *El Plumier* and the *Royal Admiral*, arrived independently at Hauraki in March 1801 to obtain spars.

Most if not all of these Hauraki spars would have been kahikatea. Kauri did not grow on the extensive swampy flats visited by the tree fellers up the Waihou River at the head of the Hauraki Gulf (see Kauri spars at Trafalgar, page 61). Before long, buyers in China, India, and Port Jackson realised the non-durable kahikatea was unsuitable for spars, and the Waihou was abandoned as a source of suitable timber.

It is uncertain when kauri first became a component of the spar cargoes. By the first decade of the nineteenth century, increasing numbers of sealing and whaling ships were calling in at the Bay of Islands for supplies, mainly under the patronage of Te Pahi, an influential chief of the northern Bay of Islands alliance (later Nga Puhi) whose dealings with New South Wales Governor King had done much to ease such transactions. Many of these ships loaded small deck cargoes of spar timber to supplement their sealskins and whale oil. Some of these spars may have been kauri.

Ships seeking spars in the Bay relied on local people to guide them to suitable trees. The most extensive forests containing kauri were those in the south-east hinterland (behind Manawaora and in the catchments of the Waikare and Kawakawa Inlets) and inland between Lake Omapere and the Hokianga. In most of the heavily populated coastal areas, including around Te Puna and the Purerua Peninsula where Te Pahi lived, the forests had long been cleared and the land was covered with scrub and head-high bracken fern. Kauri stands would not have been as accessible as kahikatea, the dominant tree growing on the river flats and by appearance equally suitable for spars.

Two ships, the *Commerce* (in 1807) and the *City of Edinburgh* (in 1809), were recorded as loading unspecified 'pine logs and spars' from the Bay. Berry and Pattison of the *City of Edinburgh* were taken by chiefs Tara and Tupi of the southern Bay of Islands alliance to 'the timber district' up a creek near Kawakawa where some spars cut earlier had been abandoned. At the end of a three-month stay, the ship left on an unsuccessful voyage to Fiji for sandalwood, then returned to complete its spar cargo at Kororareka (now Russell). It has been suggested that the speed with which the Kororareka people not only felled trees, but also trimmed and squared the logs, then

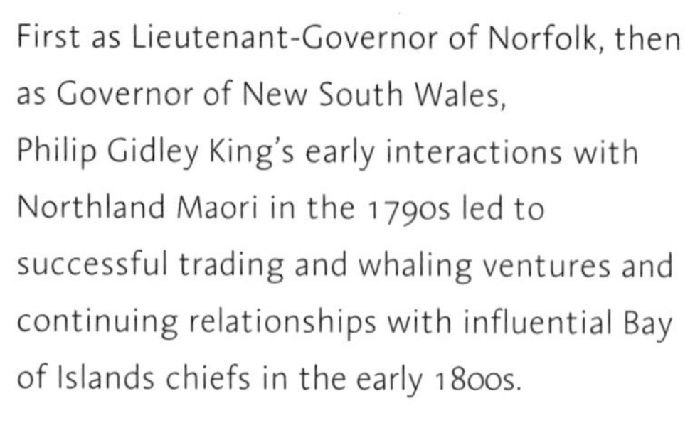

First as Lieutenant-Governor of Norfolk, then as Governor of New South Wales, Philip Gidley King's early interactions with Northland Maori in the 1790s led to successful trading and whaling ventures and continuing relationships with influential Bay of Islands chiefs in the early 1800s.

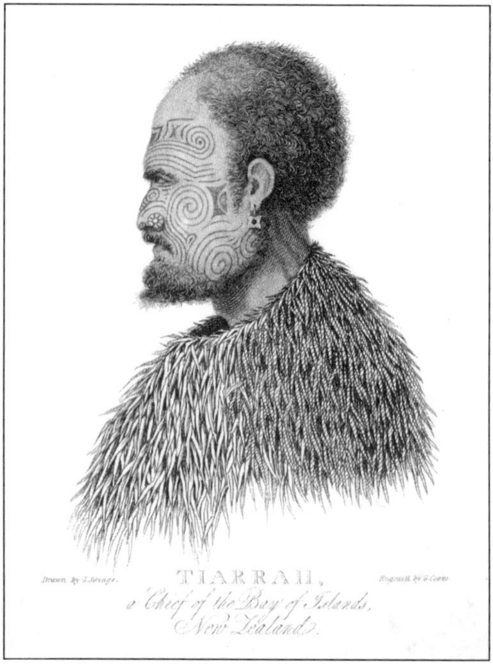

The Whangaroa chief Te Ara (George), who was the trigger for the attack on the *Boyd* in 1809, drawn by John Savage in 1807.

rafted them down the river indicates that these were probably the more accessible kahikatea. However, as the timber-seeking missionary Marsden was a few years later taken to accessible kauri stands twenty kilometres or so upstream from the Kawakawa Inlet and obtained several cargoes of kauri spars from the Bay's timber districts, the *City of Edinburgh*'s logs may well have included kauri.

Spar seekers were certainly being taken to stands of kauri at that time, as revealed by a Maori account of the fate of the spar party from the *Boyd* at Whangaroa in 1809:

> *Tara [Te Ara of Ngati Uru] told the following to us, . . . they invited the people of the ship to go and look at a kauri forest at the head of the Whanga-roa harbour where the Maori killed all those who went to look at the forest . . . .*
>
> (Salmond 1997, from a John White manuscript)

KAURI SPARS AT TRAFALGAR?

Popular opinion claims that kauri spars were fitted to HMS *Victory*, commanded by Admiral Lord Nelson at the 1805 Battle of Trafalgar. But taking a pocket knife to *Victory*'s present masts would provide no clue. Her masts and spars suffered extensive damage during the battle and were replaced in a major refit at the Chatham dockyards in 1806.

Small amounts of kauri may well have reached Port Jackson earlier than 1805 — G. F. Angus reported that seven ships had arrived there with New Zealand timber by 1796 — but there is no evidence that this timber reached official naval buyers. Apparent records of kauri being taken from Great Barrier Island and possibly the Coromandel in the early 1790s for the navy have now been discredited as the yarns of an enthusiastic but unreliable amateur maritime historian, Forbes Eady, published in the 1930s.

Although the *Royal Admiral* delivered a load of spars to the naval authorities in China after its 1801 visit to Hauraki, these were unlikely to have been kauri. Timber cut from the same trees and offloaded at Tahiti for houses rotted within five years. Captain Wilson himself noted that the timber seemed unsuitable for naval use, but persisted with felling trees as the logs would be useful for other purposes. Where these trees were felled on the banks of the Waihou River, a sawmill established in 1868 milled about 4700 cubic metres of kahikatea every year for forty years — no other timber species were present.

Perhaps further exploration of early ship records from the appropriate time, both for those purported to have obtained kauri spar cargoes and for naval ships requiring refits, would provide the definitive answer. Until then, the use of kauri spars at Trafalgar remains attractive conjecture.

HMS *Victory*, which served as Admiral Lord Nelson's flagship at the Battle of Trafalgar in 1805.

The spar party from the *Boyd* were taken by Ngati Uru to this kauri grove at Kaeo, beyond the head of the Whangaroa Harbour, where they were killed. The attack on the ship followed.

Exchanges and engagements

The Hauraki people had not hesitated to engage with the East India Company ships that arrived in search of spars in the 1790s. Large numbers of Maori visited the ships, eager for iron and intensely curious. They slept on board, shared meals, provided food and flax, guided the tree fellers into the forest, and assisted in the hauling of logs to the ships. In return they received the desired iron tools and axes. Relationships stayed mostly amicable. Despite the occasional skirmish, misunderstandings were soon resolved in the face of the mutual benefits.

By 1809, exchanges with the sealers and whalers who visited the Bay of Islands were often less amicable. Many of the crews were ex-convicts, often violent and undisciplined, and their captains were not much better. Young Maori men were sometimes kidnapped to replace crew; others voluntarily joined the ships in search of adventure. Some were ill-treated or abandoned on foreign shores, despite attempts from the Governor in Sydney to prohibit such behaviour. At the same time, attitudes towards the 'savages' on shore became increasingly objectionable, with refusals to pay for supplies, plundering of crops, and rough handling of any chiefs who objected (thereby desecrating their tapu and undermining their mana).

Retaliatory raids against offending ships culminated with the 1809 attack on the *Boyd*. Whangaroa inhabitants, Ngati Pou and Ngati Uru, had previously sworn to attack the next ship to arrive in retaliation for a ship-borne epidemic that had earlier decimated their numbers. Alerted by rumours that a crew had indeed been killed, Berry (still loading spars on the *City of Edinburgh* at Kororareka) reached Whangaroa to find that the *Boyd* had been plundered and burnt to the waterline — an inadvertent engagement with gunpowder. The locals, having dined on their victims, were now wearing their clothing and boasting of their actions.

During his investigation, Berry was misled by the similar names Te Puhi (a Ngati Uru chief at Whangaroa) and Te Pahi (the influential northern alliance chief), and blamed the latter for initiating the attack. He was no doubt encouraged to do so by the Whangaroa chiefs — allies of southern Bay of Islands chiefs Tupi and Tara (who were still with Berry) and rivals of Te Pahi. Later investigations largely exonerated Te Pahi from direct personal involvement. Various Maori accounts agreed that when the *Boyd* called at Whangaroa for a load of kauri spars, Ngati Uru chiefs Pipikoitareke and his son Te Puhi attacked and killed the crew in retaliation for the flogging of Te Ara (Pipi's younger son, known as George), who had been on a whaling voyage with the ship. After killing the spar party in the kauri forest, they had gone on to kill the rest of the crew on board. Te Pahi, arriving late on the scene, had tried to rescue some sailors clinging to the rigging, but they were caught and killed in the water before they could swim towards his canoe.

Berry's reports resulted in Te Pahi being labelled a treacherous cannibal who had bitten — and eaten — the hands that fed him. As a result, a party of incensed whalers later attacked and destroyed Te Pahi's village at Te Puna, wounding him and killing many others. Antagonism between Te Pahi and the chiefs at Whangaroa escalated to warfare, during which Te Pahi was finally killed. The people at Whangaroa in 1809 were those displaced from the Bay of Islands after Marion du Fresne's visit in 1772, and Te Pahi had connections to Te Kauri's people, the infiltrating Nga Puhi. The ripples of retaliation had not yet subsided.

With this incident and its aftermath, the increasingly uneasy exchanges between visiting ships and local people came to a head. The attraction of calling into the Bay for spar cargoes, whether kauri or kahikatea, lost its appeal for some years.

INTREPID MAORI TRAVELLERS

Bay of Islands Maori soon seized opportunities to travel on whaling ships beyond New Zealand's shores. By 1810, Maori travellers had already visited ports in the Pacific, India, Malaysia, England, and South America, as well as Port Jackson. Some of them returned to develop significant relationships with visiting Europeans. In the 1790s, Governor King's crucial liaison with northern Bay of Islands chief Te Pahi had created mutual opportunities for trade. This was followed in the early nineteenth century by equally significant liaisons between Church Missionary Society missionary Marsden, Ruatara, and Hongi Hika (Te Pahi's successors) that created the first opportunities for European settlement.

Northern Bay of Islands chief Te Pahi was the first influential chief to visit New South Wales, where he and his sons were guests of Governor King in 1805. Convinced of the benefits of association with Europeans, interested in their technology and agriculture, and curious about their religion, Te Pahi returned to the Bay of Islands with iron tools, livestock, seed potatoes and fruit trees, and an agreement to allow the establishment of the first Church Missionary Society mission under his patronage.

Having spent four years on whaling ships, Ruatara left England in 1809 on the same ship as Marsden, who invited the young chief to stay at Parramatta. Ruatara then returned to the Bay of Islands as Te Pahi's successor. His European goods and experience, his surreal stories of horse-drawn carriages, and his insistence that wheat was the unlikely source of ship's biscuit met with mixed reception. But when Marsden at last sent him a steel hand-mill on the *Active*'s first visit in 1814, Ruatara, with a dramatic flourish, ground some grain from his disparaged wheat crop and baked up a 'cake' in a frying pan. He won instant converts among his audience of influential chiefs.

After further study at Parramatta, Ruatara took the new mission in the Bay of Islands under his protection, no doubt feeling obligation or loyalty to Marsden. He planned extensive wheat cultivations as a new food crop and trade resource for his people and marked out a European-style town near Te Puna. When he unexpectedly died of respiratory illness a few months later, early in 1815, his role as protector of missionaries and promoter of new crops was continued by Hongi Hika, a northern alliance chief.

It was Hongi Hika who made the most capital out of travel, trade, and new technology. His astute purchase of muskets from whaling ships (paid for with potatoes grown for the purpose) initially gave him an advantage in skirmishes with related but rival northern chiefs that had had their origins in the aftermath of Marion du Fresne's visit in 1772. At the same time, his enviable monopoly of the European mission stations at Rangihoua, Kerikeri, and later at Waimate increased competitive tension and triggered the first campaigns of the Musket Wars (see Chapter 4, Maori dynamics and the Musket Wars).

When rival northern chiefs achieved similar quantities of muskets in a nineteenth-century arms race, Hongi upped the status stakes by travelling to England in 1820. There, with the help of Church Missionary Society missionary and admirer Thomas Kendall, he met King George IV, studied at Cambridge, and dined in high society, achieving his aim of acquiring muskets and mana in the process. In Sydney on his way home, he exchanged gifts for more guns and arrived back in the Bay of Islands in 1821 with at least 400 muskets. Armed with awe-inspiring firepower, Hongi won the cooperation of the other Bay alliances in a new round of campaigns that secured Nga Puhi dominance in the north but resulted in his own death from a chest wound in 1828.

Ruatara, Te Pahi's young successor, stands beside Samuel Marsden as his translator in this reconstruction of Marsden's first service at Rangihoua, Bay of Islands, on Christmas Day in 1814. Like Ruatara, Hongi Hika and Korokoro (another Bay chief), depicted here standing at the head of their men, are dressed in the uniforms given to them by Governor Macquarie in Sydney.

Chapter 4

Ships and shore stations

ESTABLISHMENT OF THE TIMBER TRADE, 1810–1840

The right stuff

Anchored off Kororareka, the brig lies surrounded by rafts of floating kauri spars. Maori in canoes with logs lashed to the sides paddle towards the ship, eager to trade. The bargaining is brisk, but three spars yield the desired axe. Many chiefs, confident in their status and vying for the now-valued contact with Europeans, clamber on board to share meals and conversation. It is early 1815. The brig is missionary Samuel Marsden's Active *on her second visit to the Bay of Islands within the year, in the process of establishing the first Church Missionary Society (CMS) site at Rangihoua.*

When Marsden sought a spar cargo to help defray the expense of setting up the mission station, local chiefs willingly took the CMS men on a grand tour of the timber districts. With the permission of southern Bay of Islands chief, Tara, they visited stands of suitable kauri up rivers at Kawakawa, Waikare, and near Paroa Bay; they went inland with Hongi Hika as far as Lake Omapere; and they sailed to the Hauraki Gulf and Whangarei Harbour with Ruatara (see Chapter 3, Intrepid Maori travellers). By the end of their stay, all these

Samuel Marsden first arrived in northern New Zealand waters in 1814 with several Maori chiefs on board from Sydney, including Hongi Hika and Ruatara. This engraving, based on a sketch by John Nicholas, who accompanied the missionaries, shows the brig *Active* at North Cape surrounded by Maori canoes, their crews eager to visit and trade.

Bay of Islands chiefs were honouring promises to provide flax, spars, and timber for building the mission houses in return for axes and other trade goods.

Marsden returned to Sydney in February 1815, leaving behind him at Rangihoua the beginnings of the first European settlement in the north. The *Active* was to return frequently over the next few years, each time leaving with cargoes of dressed flax, kauri spars, and sawn timber — Marsden seemed as committed to commerce as to converts.

Essential liaisons with influential chiefs set the pattern for continued European exploration of New Zealand harbours and the establishment of settlements or trading ventures in the first forty years of the nineteenth century. But if Europeans were dependent

In this reconstruction, Samuel Marsden and his companions greet some Maori chiefs on their landing at the Bay of Islands in December 1814.

on Maori for provisions, a place to set up, and protection, the Maori chiefs were becoming dependent on Europeans for the trade goods that now featured in maintaining the balance of wealth and mana. This mutual dependence increased tolerance on both sides — encounters were smoothed by the oil of commerce.

Quick to absorb desirable elements of the European lifestyle, Maori adapted them for their own purposes. Before long, it was the chiefs who dictated the terms of trade. By the time of Marsden's visits, hoop-iron and nails had been replaced by a demand for axes and implements. As the chiefs grew familiar with European manners and lost their fear of muskets, firearms became the preferred item of trade. Ownership of muskets and association with Europeans became essential new components in the Maori system of exchange and reciprocity. These components intensified the traditional rivalry between chiefs and contributed to a temporary escalation of the scale of ongoing conflicts.

The early establishment of the kauri timber trade took place against this background of increasing conflict — the Musket Wars — that changed the patterns of people and power throughout the country and largely dictated the direction taken by European settlement in New Zealand.

Sticks of first rate quality

The kauri spars taken to Port Jackson on the *Active* in 1814 and Marsden's reassurances of friendly dealings with Maori renewed interest in New Zealand as a source of timber. In 1820, two British navy store ships (the *Dromedary* and the *Coromandel*) arrived in New Zealand looking for cargoes of spars, preferably kauri, as an alternative to paying heavy government duties on Baltic timber.

The *Dromedary* was sporting the earliest confirmed kauri spar used by the navy. Cut as a mast for the whaler *Catherine*, probably by carpenter William Hall at the CMS mission in 1817, this spar had been bought for the *Dromedary*. Major Richard Cruise, in charge of a detachment of sixty soldiers on board the *Dromedary*, reports in his journal:

> *It was well tried during its return to its native country, and proved itself to be, in seamen's phrase, a* stick *of first rate quality.*
>
> (Cruise 1827)

The schooner *Prince Regent*, sailing as tender to the *Dromedary* on its search for kauri spars in 1820, was the first European ship to enter the Waitemata and Hokianga Harbours.

Pulled by the *Dromedary*'s bullocks, this plough was the first to till agricultural land in New Zealand — at the Kerikeri mission station.

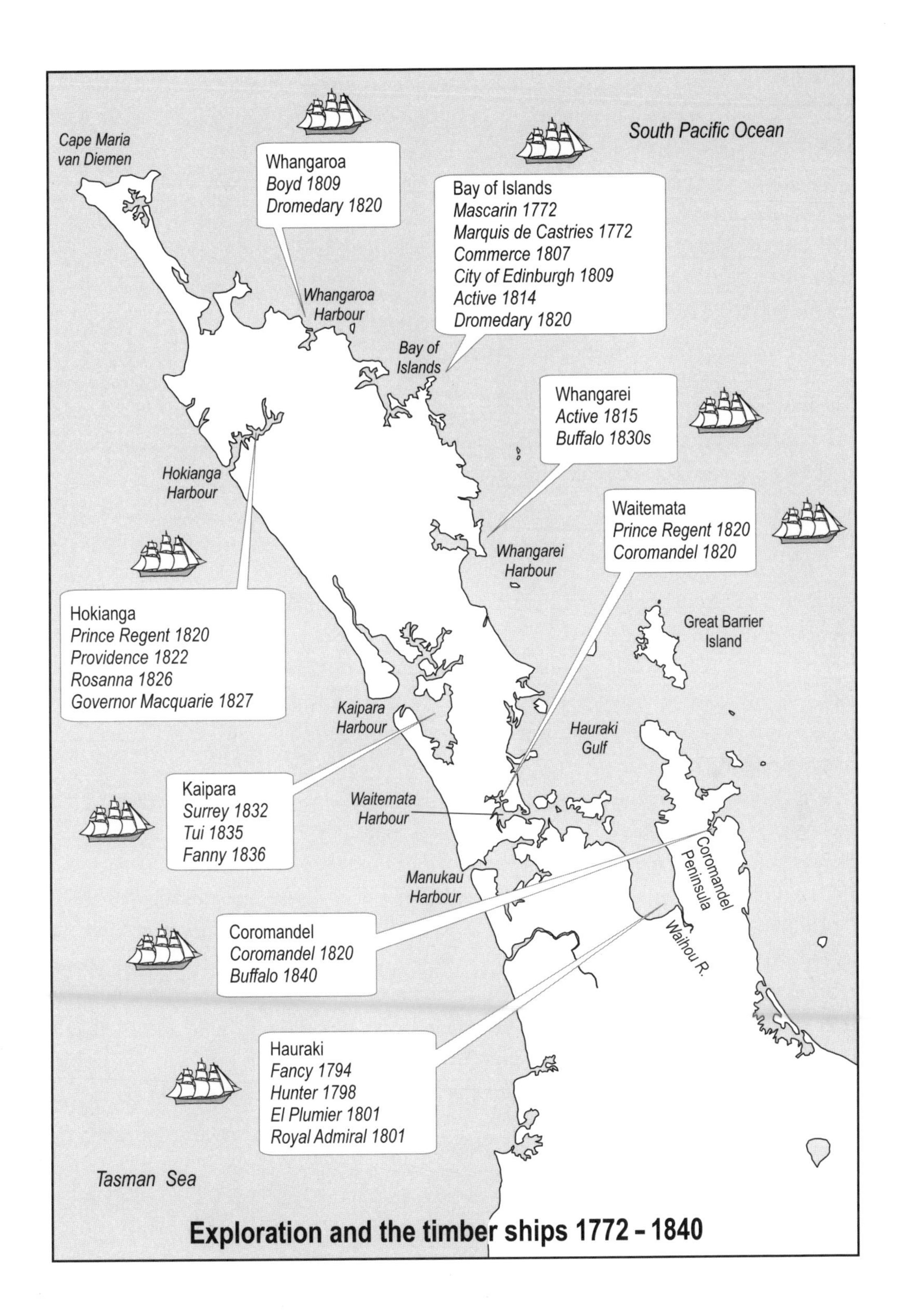
South Pacific Ocean
Cape Maria van Diemen
Whangaroa
Boyd 1809
Dromedary 1820
Bay of Islands
Mascarin 1772
Marquis de Castries 1772
Commerce 1807
City of Edinburgh 1809
Active 1814
Dromedary 1820
Whangaroa Harbour
Bay of Islands
Whangarei
Active 1815
Buffalo 1830s
Hokianga Harbour
Waitemata
Prince Regent 1820
Coromandel 1820
Whangarei Harbour
Hokianga
Prince Regent 1820
Providence 1822
Rosanna 1826
Governor Macquarie 1827
Great Barrier Island
Kaipara Harbour
Hauraki Gulf
Kaipara
Surrey 1832
Tui 1835
Fanny 1836
Waitemata Harbour
Coromandel Peninsula
Manukau Harbour
Coromandel
Coromandel 1820
Buffalo 1840
Waihou R.
Hauraki
Fancy 1794
Hunter 1798
El Plumier 1801
Royal Admiral 1801
Tasman Sea
Exploration and the timber ships 1772 – 1840

In Sydney, as well as Major Cruise's soldiers and the services of the schooner *Prince Regent* as tender, the *Dromedary* took on board one missionary (Samuel Marsden, to facilitate the required 'friendly disposition of the natives'), two timber carriages (for hauling out the felled spars), nine 'New Zealanders' (chiefs or their sons who had been with Marsden at Parramatta, some to learn the rudiments of European farming, others 'to obtain muskets and gunpowder, or merely to gratify their rambling disposition'), and twelve bullocks. The navy's first expedition to obtain kauri spars was thus prepared for all contingencies.

At the Bay of Islands, the naval party were first taken up the Waikare by Titore (the northern alliance chief at Waimate and on board from Sydney). To their disappointment and Titore's, 'no cowry trees, of the size of those the *Dromedary* was instructed to bring home were to be found'. The Kawakawa forests proved equally disappointing. Cruise's words do not imply the absence of kauri, merely the absence of trees big enough for naval purposes. Smaller kauri spars seem to have been extracted here previously for Marsden (see also Chapter 3, Kahikatea to kauri).

Marsden had visited the Hokianga Harbour on board the *General Gates* the previous year, and reported suitable kauri there in great abundance. A small reconnaissance party set off overland from the new CMS mission station at Kerikeri, where Hall had built a two-storeyed house from heart kauri in 1819. Still standing, Kemp House is the oldest surviving wooden house in New Zealand. While the reconnaissance party was away, the *Prince Regent* continued to explore possible sources of kauri in the Bay and beyond. Explorations along the east coast to Bream Head also proved frustrating, with no safe anchorages where timber was found. The most promising source of accessible tall kauri spars was undoubtedly the Hokianga.

On their second attempt to take the ships around Cape Maria Van Diemen to the Hokianga, Captain Kent and the *Prince Regent* successfully crossed the bar, but Captain Skinner was reluctant to risk the deeper draft of the *Dromedary*. After taking soundings, the ships returned to the east coast — to the disappointment of the waiting Hokianga people.

Deciding to settle for kahikatea spars from Kawakawa, the naval party negotiated an agreed price of one axe per spar with Te Koki, the local southern alliance chief. Labour relations proved difficult. Recalcitrant Maori workmen felled trees on the wrong side of the river (those marked by the ship's carpenter were probably in some other chief's jurisdiction), cut spars short, stole axes and tackle, argued over pay, and constantly knocked off work to attend funerals and plant kumara. Two months later, the operation had yielded only eighteen usable spars.

In the meantime, the Ngati Uru chief Te Ara prevailed upon Captain Skinner to try Whangaroa. Encouraged by assurances of suitable kauri and the indefinite suspension of work at Kawakawa, the *Dromedary* abandoned all but four of the kahikatea spars and set sail for Whangaroa.

On board were the bullocks, re-embarked from the Kerikeri mission station where they had achieved the first ploughing of agricultural land in New Zealand. Over the next four winter months they were to earn their keep. Although kauri overhung the Kaeo River, those of proper size were some distance away and in difficult terrain. Each spar took up to two days to retrieve. After being winched by capstan out of a deep ravine, the spars had to be hauled to the water's edge by the bullocks. For this purpose, the spar party built a road 'a mile and a quarter long, over a clay surface, which could not be kept in repair in bad weather'. This road crossed swamps 'filled up with fascines' to create a solid base and negotiated a bridge built over 'a deep and rapid brook'.

The Maori labourers were reluctant to help with hauling the spars, although they proved excellent tree fellers. Maybe their keen sense of status made them baulk, either at being equated with bullocks or because of the perceived slave status of the convict bullock drivers. But the efforts of the bullocks in pulling the timber carriages excited much Maori attention:

> *People from distant parts of the country came to witness the extraordinary spectacle and returned with the most exaggerated accounts of the karaddee nue [kararehe nui], or large dogs, the white men had landed on their island.*
>
> (Cruise 1827)

Getting the price right

Progress was impeded by more urgent Maori agendas — for example, September was the time for drying fish and planting potatoes. Progress was also punctuated by continual violent outbursts from Te Ara; frequent strikes called by him and Te Puhi (the senior Ngati Uru chief), suspicious that once the ship was loaded, retribution for their attack on the *Boyd* would be imminent; rivalry between them and Te Pere, who was offering kauri from Ngati Pou land elsewhere in Whangaroa Harbour; and raids from related rival chiefs and those further north — part of the growing intensity of exchanges that escalated into the Musket Wars.

At the same time, the naval party had to endure the frustration of taking second place to any visiting whaling ship. Approved naval trade goods were no match for the muskets and powder willingly traded by whaling ships:

> *While our men were doomed to live ten months on salt provisions, we had the mortification of seeing the crews of other ships refreshed with as much pork as they could consume. . . . the islanders, with their canoes filled with hogs, triumphantly passed us by, and remarked that King George's people [the navy] were, with regard to their fire-arms, the stingiest they had ever met.*
>
> (Cruise 1827)

Not only the Ngati Uru chiefs were dissatisfied with the price. When the two store ships eventually arrived back in England in 1821 with combined cargoes of 200 kauri spars (the *Coromandel* having with equal difficulty loaded kauri near Waiau on the peninsula that later took the ship's name), the navy decided that the cost and time of direct extraction was prohibitive. Although kauri spars continued to be used for naval purposes after 1820, they were bought mostly from traders.

One of the last notable naval supply ships to visit the kauri timber districts was the *Buffalo*, which took her spar cargoes from Whangaroa Harbour, Mahurangi, and Tutukaka in the 1830s before being wrecked near Whitianga on the Coromandel coast in 1840. In 1834, the Waimate chief Titore acted as her agent, honouring at last his promise to provide kauri spars for the navy. The purchase completed, he dictated the following letter:

> *To the King of England, King William.*
> *Here am I, the friend of Captain Saddler. The ship is full and now about to sail. I have heard that you aforetime were the Captain of a ship. Do you, therefore, examine the spars, whether they are good or whether they are bad. Should you and the French quarrel, here are some trees for your battle ships. I have put on board the* Buffalo *a greenstone battle-axe, and two garments. These are all the things which the New Zealanders possess. If I had anything better, I would give it to Captain Saddler for you. This is all mine to you.*
>
> (Halkett and Sale 1986)

Maori assumptions of chiefly equality with kings and governors, together with the exchange of gifts as an expression of status, had not changed. In response, King William IV sent Titore an ancient suit of chain mail — the irony of his choice of a reciprocal gift of handsome but now superseded military value may have been unintentional.

Footholds on shore

In 1827, the *Governor Macquarie*, commanded by Captain Kent, arrived at Horeke, where the first timber and shipbuilding enterprise in the Hokianga had been established. Artist Augustus Earle, a passenger on board, noted:

> *. . . a snug little colony of our own countrymen, comfortably settled and usefully employed in this savage and unexplored country. Some enterprising merchants of Port Jackson have established here a dockyard and a number of sawpits. Several vessels have been laden with timber and spars; one vessel has been built,*

> *launched, and sent to sea from this spot; and another of a hundred and fifty tons burthen was then upon the stocks!*
>
> (Earle 1832)

Downstream at Koutu Point, where the *Governor Macquarie* had anchored for a few days, Kent had been putting his earlier exploration of the Hokianga on the *Prince Regent* into good use. He had established the first trading station in New Zealand there in 1826, building on his good relationship with western Nga Puhi chief Moetara from nearby Pakanae — and his sister Wharo, who became Kent's wife. Trading muskets for salt pork, potatoes, and 'pine logs', Kent's station at Koutu led the way for other traders looking to establish flax and timber ventures in the north as the southern sealing trade declined.

Also on board the *Governor Macquarie* was a party of Wesleyan missionaries. Ousted from Whangaroa in 1826 after skirmishes between northern alliance chief Hongi Hika and local chiefs, the Wesleyans had been invited to set up their mission in the Hokianga by Patuone, another western Nga Puhi chief eager to gain the advantages offered by Europeans. Under Patuone's protection, John Hobbs and his fellow Wesleyans eventually settled at Mangungu, where they left the legacy of another historic kauri house (built in 1838).

Not content with protection and patronage, the newly arrived traders and missionaries sought to buy land for their ventures. Kent himself had paid for land at Koutu with muskets, powder, and other goods. In the same year, Captain Herd of the *Rosanna* paid £20,000 for land he bought from Maori chiefs in the Hokianga, at Hauraki, on Waiheke Island, and in the Manukau Harbour. These purchases were on behalf of the New Zealand Company of 1825, which intended settling colonists to process timber and dress flax. Nothing came of such intentions, but these 1826 land purchases signalled a significant change from ship-based trading visits to shore-based permanent settlements. Europeans were here to stay.

Timber stations and pit-sawyers

Horeke (known as Deptford to the thirty English mill hands and shipwrights settled there) had been established in 1826 by Sydney merchants Thomas Raine, David Ramsay, and Gordon Browne. By the time Augustus Earle arrived on the *Governor Macquarie*, ships from Sydney were already calling for loads of kauri spars and sawn timber. The ship he saw on the stocks was the *New Zealander*, one of the first to be built of kauri (see Chapter 5, Sailing ships and shipbuilders).

From Horeke in 1827, Earle and his companions continued by canoe up the Waihou River, then followed the Maori route overland to the Bay of Islands. Where the river narrowed, they came across four Scots pit-sawyers 'busily employed in cutting timber, sawing planks, and making oars for the Sydney market'. These men were living and working under the protection of Patuone, who had a 'splendid village very near the carpenters' establishment . . .'. Staunch individualists, they had stayed behind when Captain Herd abandoned both the land he bought at Rawene (known as Herd's Point for many years) and any idea of leaving his party of sixty prospective colonists there.

At this time, the Hokianga chiefs were under threat of outside attack. Herd may have been daunted by over-vigorous displays of strength from warriors preparing for battle, a marked contrast to his friendly reception in 1822 by chiefs flushed with victory after the first major campaigns of the Musket Wars. In that year he had successfully taken the first timber ship across the Hokianga bar. The *Providence* had left for South America with a full cargo of kauri spars of various sizes, obtained with ease from local Maori without any of the hassles experienced by the *Dromedary* at Whangaroa two years earlier.

Herd need not have worried. Local Maori now realised that the advantages of access to Europeans — or Pakeha as they had become known — far outweighed any disadvantages. Leading chiefs in the Hokianga went out of their way to protect the growing number of missions and timber stations in their territories against any outside threat. Such protection included Moetara first shifting his village nearer the *Rosanna*'s Scots when they moved down to Pakanae, then in 1833 shifting everyone to Captain William Young's sawmilling station at Koutu, where he surrounded both Maori and Pakeha houses with fortifications. Patuone and his brother Nene even intervened in a dispute over pay between Captain Crowe of the *Bristol Packet* and the pit-sawyers he had employed to provide a cargo of sawn timber in the early 1830s. In what became known as the 'Battle of the Plank', the chiefs backed the hundred or so local Pakeha who came armed to support the aggrieved pit-sawyers. The potentially ugly altercation dissipated in hot air and smoke as the disputed timber stacks were set on fire and destroyed.

Horeke, the first of the kauri timber ventures, had a chequered history despite its auspicious beginning. Failing in 1829, it was then bought at auction in Sydney by Thomas McDonnell, one of several enterprising and sometimes competing timber merchants who settled in the Hokianga during the 1830s. The harbour's accessible kauri forests continued to attract ships and pit-sawyers in increasing numbers, despite the difficulties of crossing the bar. This crossing was to claim several ships and many lives before John Martin (Captain Kent's mate, who had also settled in the Hokianga with his Maori wife, Kati) acted as pilot after 1832. These early timber stations and the sawyers who settled on the harbour's shores signalled the beginning of more than fifty years of intensive timber extraction from the Hokianga.

A view of the Hokianga sketched by trader Joel Polack about 1835 shows a fenced Maori burial ground, canoes on the harbour, and European buildings on the point in the background.

Conquering the Kaipara

Encouraged by the ease of extracting kauri from the Hokianga, timber traders in the early 1830s also turned their attention to the vast forests that surrounded the labyrinth of the Kaipara Harbour further south. Although the inexhaustible Samuel Marsden had twice visited the Kaipara on foot in 1820, the shifting sand bars and treacherous currents of the harbour entrance had been considered too hazardous for sailing ships.

Several contenders vie for the prize of being the first to negotiate the harbour entrance. In 1832, trader and adventurer Captain Ranulph Dacre is said to have taken the *Surrey* through the entrance to obtain kauri spars. Late in 1835 or early in 1836, depending on which contender is favoured, Hokianga timber merchant Thomas McDonnell on board the *Tui* (Captain Lawreston) and his arch-rival Wesleyan missionary William White from Mangungu on board the *Fanny* (Captain Wing) both claimed with some vehemence to have been the first to negotiate a sea passage into the Kaipara.

What is certain is that by the early 1840s, traders and ships were braving the entrance in search of spar cargoes, and missionaries and colonial agents were assessing the potential of the Kaipara for settlement. Maori chiefs accustomed to trade were quick to capitalise. One such chief, Parore Te Awha (a Nga Puhi relative of Te Roroa), who had traded timber in the Hokianga, moved to Kaihu and the Northern Wairoa about 1836. He may have done so partly to enhance his prospects in the timber trade — he was also involved in sales of Kaipara land to Pakeha at this time.

Counteracting the perils of the harbour entrance were the advantages of seemingly endless supplies of accessible kauri timber and chiefs willing to sell land, tracts of which had been temporarily deserted by Ngati Whatua after their defeat by Nga Puhi in the Musket Wars. In 1845, German naturalist Ernest Dieffenbach reported his findings on the Kaipara Harbour back to the Wakefield Land Company:

> *I am not acquainted with any place in New Zealand where [kauri trees] are more plentiful, of greater height and diameter, and of easier access. . . . Timber is likewise found on the banks of all . . . tributaries . . . and everywhere there is suitable land to enable the colonist to combine agricultural pursuits with the timber trade, in which case alone, the latter can prove profitable in New Zealand.*
>
> (Ryburn 1999)

A new era was about to begin in which a now fully fledged kauri timber trade dominated the economy of an emerging colony.

Competition, kauri, and commerce

By the time Augustus Earle visited the Hokianga in 1827, Maori attitudes towards kauri had changed dramatically. Traditionally, kauri as a tree with low 'economic value' did not feature much in the ordinary lives of Maori people (see Chapter 1, Forays into the forest). But fifty years after Marion du Fresne's first attempt to extract kauri spars, Maori were heavily involved in felling kauri and dragging the logs out of the bush. Quick to pick up new skills and adapt old, Maori workmen soon featured in all aspects of the developing kauri extraction industry, and continued to do so throughout its history. Such a major switch in attitude needs examining.

At first, Maori chiefs would have seen the receipt of goods in return for directing early Europeans to suitable kauri for spars as a gift exchange between people of equal status. As kauri rickers were of no use to Maori, the chiefs no doubt considered they got the better of the deal. Maori agendas, such as food gathering, took precedence over providing spars for Europeans, so that the early spar parties often had 'trouble with the natives'.

Maori became adept at felling kauri and dragging the logs out of the bush, often in the interests of trading for muskets.

By 1818, the concept of trading was well established. In the Bay of Islands, Maori were growing produce specifically for trade and delivering loads of timber. Marsden's commercial cargoes that year included '. . . six thousand feet of planks [fourteen cubic metres] sawn by the natives themselves and paid for with articles of husbandry . . .' (McNab 1908). When the desired item of trade became muskets, attitudes changed further. If muskets and competitive advantage could be gained by providing Europeans with kauri logs, the ever pragmatic chiefs did not hesitate to do so.

In the Hokianga in particular, kauri had become the main currency for trade by 1827:

> *While we lay here the ship* Harmony *. . . arrived from Sydney for a cargo of spars. . . . when the chiefs . . . had seen the fine double-barrelled guns and store of powder to be given as payment for the wished-for freight, they hastened to the woods, and the axe was soon laid to the roots of the trees. I saw them pursuing their laborious employ with alacrity. In a few days a sufficient number of logs came floating down the river to load the ship . . . the chief things to induce these people to work are firearms and powder; these are two stimulants to their industry which never fail.*
>
> (Earle 1832)

And so the status of the kauri in the Maori world had changed from low to high economic value, and provision of logs in exchange for muskets now came high on the Maori agenda. John Klaricich supports this interpretation of kauri's changed status:

> *It was only in that transitional period that kauri was used. It was all to do with getting muskets. That's why our northern tribes became all-powerful for that short time. Waaka Vercoe from the Tauranga region said to me, '. . . it was all right for you [Hokianga] people, you could cut down one little kauri sapling and you'd get two or three muskets — we had to cut twenty tons of flax'. Kauri was a tradeable item, it was readily accessible, and the rickers mostly required were easily manageable.*

From a modern Maori perspective, the traditional attitude towards kauri had been temporarily skewed by the intensity of the Musket Wars. But by the time the tide of war receded from the north in the early 1830s, the previous dominance of the Maori world had ebbed with the tide. The kauri timber industry was in full spate, and the kauri forests around the harbour were already being depleted. Both the natural and human landscapes of the north were facing change on a massive and irreversible scale.

Opposite Traditional skills became adapted to the unfamiliar materials of the new land. Maori weavers learned to value flax as their main textile plant, fashioning items that ranged from food baskets, nets, and cordage to everyday clothing and finely woven ceremonial cloaks.
(Chapter 1, A new land)

Below Warriors assembled on a beach in the Bay of Islands being addressed by one of their chiefs. This war party was sketched by Augustus Earle in 1828 as they waited for suitable conditions to sail on a hostile visit to Hauraki.
(Chapter 1, Cooperation and competition)

Framed by a wealth of foliage texture and shape, the light-reflecting trunk of Tane Mahuta, the largest living New Zealand kauri, soars skywards. **(Chapter 2, Kauri, king of kings)**

The interior of kauri forest is characterised by a rich mix of small trees (like taraire, tawa, and tanekaha) and shrubs amidst a dense ground layer of 'kauri grass' (actually a lily), sedge, and the scrambling liane kiekie (far left foreground). **(Chapter 2, Community and companions)**

Left This grove of young kauri trees near Auckland shows the more typical conifer form of tapering trunk, whorls of short branches, and triangular crown retained by kauri for fifty or so years. The taller older trees behind are beginning to shed their lower branches, and the tree in the right background is developing the more rounded crown of mature kauri.
Right The massive crowns of kauri provide a home for many different perching or epiphytic plants, like these lilies, creating roof gardens high above the forest canopy.

A mature kauri continually sheds its outer bark in thick plate-like scales, which prevents climbing or perching plants (epiphytes) from finding a permanent foothold. The rippled patterns range from scroll-like swirls reminiscent of Maori tattoo to hammered discs like those of beaten bronze. **(Chapter 2, Kauri, king of kings)**

Young kauri foliage, thick and leathery, longer and more pointed than adult foliage, showing its distinctive colour. Young trees have blue-green or bronze foliage, both colorations being normal for healthy trees. **(Chapter 2)**

Left The blue-green female cones of kauri take three years to ripen and shed their brown winged seeds. Their globe shape and overlapping spiral scales give kauri its botanical name, *Agathis* (Greek for 'a ball of string'). **(Chapter 2)**

Right The cylindrical male cones are often borne on the same branches as female cones, turning dark brown and releasing their wind-dispersed pollen after one year. **(Chapter 2)**

Most encounters between Maori and Europeans were amicable, though often coloured by cultural misunderstandings. In this reconstruction, Captain Cook explains the different purpose of small shot and bullets to a Maori chief and his companions in the Bay of Islands.

(Chapter 3, Strangers from the sea)

Increasingly acrimonious encounters between whalers and Maori culminated in the Ngati Uru attack on the *Boyd* and the killing of its crew in 1809, depicted in this reconstruction. **(Chapter 3, Exchanges and engagements)**

Hongi Hika (centre) with missionary Thomas Kendall and fellow chief Waikato on his visit to England in 1820. **(Chapter 3, Intrepid Maori travellers)**

Augustus Earle sketched this scene of Maori life at Pakanae village in the Hokianga during his visit on board the *Governor Macquarie* in 1827. **(Chapter 4, Footholds on shore)**

Some distance up the Waihou River on the Maori route from the Hokianga to the Bay of Islands, Augustus Earle and his companions came across Patuone's village, surrounded by kauri forest. **(Chapter 4, Timber stations and pit-sawyers)**

MAORI DYNAMICS AND THE MUSKET WARS

Manoeuvres and migrations

Uneven exposure to the new opportunities brought by Europeans temporarily tipped systems of Maori exchange and reciprocity off-balance in the early nineteenth century. Between 1818 and 1823, the rival alliances of Nga Puhi took their ongoing needs to seek utu and restore mana outside the northern region, flexing their muscles and newly acquired muskets against unrelated tribes.

Hongi Hika — northern Nga Puhi leader and first to acquire significant numbers of muskets (see Chapter 3, Intrepid Maori travellers) — succeeded in rallying rival and related chiefs into a vast northern army. Its numbers, and the deaths it inflicted, were on a scale not experienced before in Maori warfare. In varying combinations, they set out on long campaigns. Raiding as far south as Te Whanganui-a-Tara (Wellington) and east to Waikato and Heretaunga (Hawke's Bay), factions in this army used their superior firepower to settle old scores in tribal areas where chiefs had yet to acquire muskets.

The deaths incurred and the scale of the fighting meant that Hongi could not rest on his laurels. After 1825, continuing requirements to satisfy utu saw earlier allies defeated in a series of northern battles that ended only with his death in 1828. By then, Nga Puhi's resulting expansion and ascendancy in the north had triggered waves of migration that continued into the next decade. These migrations temporarily depopulated Tamaki and the Kaipara, opening

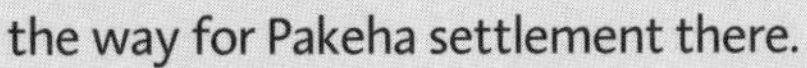

the way for Pakeha settlement there.

Defeated tribes in turn sought utu against traditional rivals in attempts to restore their damaged mana. As they too gained muskets in trade with Pakeha, they escalated the scale of their raids against less-endowed rival groups. The result was sequential waves of increased warfare that moved south, eventually influencing Maori population

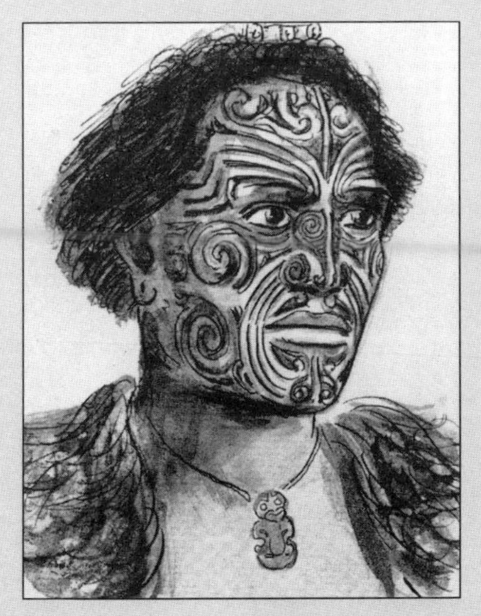

Hongi Hika, traveller, trader, and protector of Pakeha in the Bay of Islands, was leader of the northern Nga Puhi alliance and instigator of the Musket Wars. Thought to have been born in 1772, Hongi died of war wounds in 1828 at the height of his power.

Right Nene, younger brother of Patuone, became one of the leading chiefs in the Hokianga and a renowned warrior. Like his brother, he was a major patron of Pakeha traders and missionaries, taking the name Tamati Waka (Thomas Walker) when baptised in 1839. An influential signatory to the 1835 Declaration of Independence and the Treaty of Waitangi, Nene acted as intermediary and peacemaker between Hone Heke and Governors FitzRoy and Grey during the Northern War in the mid 1840s. In old age, Nene lived at Russell in a cottage built for him by the government, retaining high prestige amongst Pakeha and the administration until his death in 1871.

Left A participant in Nga Puhi's long-distance raids the length of the North Island and other campaigns in the Musket Wars, western Nga Puhi chief Patuone was a relative, rival, and sometimes uneasy ally of Hongi Hika. He became a major player in contacts between Maori and Pakeha, giving protection and patronage to timber traders and missionaries in the Hokianga in the 1820s before moving to Hauraki. Baptised in 1840, Patuone took the Pakeha name Eruera Maihi (Edward Marsh). Later, he lived in Auckland, where he was valued as advisor and friend to the Governor until he died aged over 100 in 1872.

patterns throughout New Zealand. Not until all tribes had access to arms and Pakeha traders or missionaries did these waves of war lose their impetus, people settle into their new territories, and some sort of balance become restored.

The currency of war

The escalation of Maori retaliatory raiding not only owed something to the ownership of muskets, but also to a new economic ability to sustain lengthy expeditions. Pigs and potatoes now provided surpluses to trade for muskets — and other people's potatoes could be eaten on the march.

If pigs and potatoes contributed to escalated warfare, kauri as a currency for muskets and ammunition may have hastened its subsidence in the north. Initially poor in muskets, by 1825 the Hokianga chiefs were fighting on equal terms with their relative, rival, and sometimes ally, Hongi Hika. The major involvement of Hokianga Maori in kauri extraction by the 1830s therefore probably contributed to the rapid distribution of muskets that rebalanced power among feuding northern groups and returned local hostilities to pre-musket levels.

CHAPTER 5

Hinterland and harbour

EXPANSION OF THE TIMBER INDUSTRY, 1840–1920

Getting into gear

A sailing barque waits at the wharf, ready to load. Squared logs move down the mill chute to lie in a vast floating mass, like the spilled contents of a giant's matchbox, that obscures the water below. Stacks of sawn timber rise beside the mill sheds. Pole-wielders shout from their precarious footholds on the raft of chained logs just arriving at the booms from up-river. The auxiliary schooner casts off the tow line and moves back out into the stream. Saws whine. Men sweat. Steam from the boiler drifts, obscuring the line of small wooden houses. Behind the mill, the closest hills lie stark, soot-stained, and stripped of all but scattered stumps and skeleton tree heads. It is 1875. The Aratapu mill in the Northern Wairoa is in full production.

Aratapu was the first and largest of many steam-driven timber mills scattered along the shores of the Kaipara Harbour. When it was built in 1865, the Aratapu mill represented a major shift in technology. Until then, spars or squared logs (also known as 'balk' or 'baulk') had been produced for export and pit-sawn timber for local consumption. But once the

A sailing ship loads kauri timber at Aratapu wharf around 1900. At the height of the kauri era, up to forty outward-bound ships with timber cargoes crossed the Kaipara bar each day.

pace of Pakeha settlement picked up after formal British annexation of New Zealand in 1840 (when the Treaty of Waitangi was signed, see Chapter 6, Tricks or treaties), pit-sawyers could not keep up with the demand for sawn timber — even the most skilled pair took six weeks to cut enough timber for one modest house. Machines began to replace muscle. The earliest sawmills in the kauri districts used machines that were driven by water races and waterfalls. Later, with the developments of an industrial age, saws driven by steam-boilers meant that vast amounts of timber could be cut.

As domestic demand for sawn timber increased, so did export trade — kauri logs provided useful revenue for a new and fragile colonial economy that desperately needed external markets. In the south of the colony, where pastoral sheep runs had been developed, woolpacks were traded to make fortunes for the gentlemen squatters — wool dominated exports in the 1850s. In the north, extensive tracts of forest precluded such development and the ample resources of easily millable kauri timber must have seemed heaven-sent. But setting up a sawmill was expensive, and sawdust often proved a less than solid foundation for a fortune. The success of many sawmills see-sawed through a series of financial boom–bust cycles that were to plague the industry throughout its history.

In practice, ease of access and extraction of the timber dictated the economics of kauri logging in any one area. The web of waterways that linked hinterland to harbour throughout the north was the key. Because kauri was buoyant, felled logs could be floated downstream to mills sited where wharfs could provide berths for large sailing ships. The convenience of waterways — from creek to deep-water harbour — outweighed the inconvenience of often treacherous harbour entrances. And if ships were wrecked (from the 1840s to the 1900s, about 150 came to grief on the wild west coast from Mangonui Bluff in the north to the inner Kaipara, with close to thirty at North Head alone), kauri could be used to build their replacements.

Throughout the second half of the nineteenth century, sawmillers set up production in each of the major kauri-producing areas served by deep-water harbours. Once trees close to the waterways had been felled, the extra time and expense involved in extracting trees from greater distances meant many sawmillers shipped their machines elsewhere to easier pickings. In recurring geographic boom–bust cycles, each area was subjected to intense activity until all the kauri that was economic to mill at the time had gone. Many areas were logged at least three times, each time making a profit for the contractors and the mill owners. Timber cutting shifted across the landscape and mills opened or closed as the fortunes of the industry waxed and waned in response to changing internal and external markets.

Energy and enterprise on the Hokianga

Arriving in the Hokianga in 1841, John Webster joined his older brother William at Wairere Creek, near Horeke, where he was operating the first water-driven sawmill in the harbour. In 1845, Webster enthusiastically went with Frederick Maning (Hokianga trader and in later years a Judge in the Native Land Court) to join Tamati Waka Nene's pro-government force in a fight against Hone Heke near Lake Omapere (see Chapter 6, Prestige, power, and politics). If that were not enough excitement, he accompanied John Logan Campbell of Auckland fame to San Francisco where he witnessed the great fire in 1850. On his return to the Hokianga in 1855 after further adventures, Webster took over the Kohukohu sawmill, by then the largest in the Hokianga. Webster's letters to his partner, a Sydney-based brother 'A. S.', illuminate the timber trade of the early 1860s.

Highly speculative in nature, the Kohukohu mill's profitability depended on weather, available ships (both chartered and chance arrivals), and willing buyers. Loads of spars and 'balk' often lay at the mill, waiting for the rough seas on the Hokianga bar to subside or for overdue ships to appear. Webster complained that such delays caused 'a great deal of trouble, [the timber] constantly requiring to be turned over on account of the [toredo] worm, which of late seems to be more destructive than usual'. When the chartered ships did arrive, their loading ports were sometimes too small to accommodate the available timber. Webster fretted that he would 'be left with a stock of 30 in timber [0.75 metre diameter] which is fated never to meet a market & will in time be destroyed by worm'. In a tactful brotherly rebuke, he concluded that 'we are very unfortunate in our choice of ships & I am surprised that the ports are not looked to before the vessel sails for this place'.

Webster's associated trade in goods and chattels also caused him anxiety. The goods he requested included everything imaginable — from spades, boots, and spokeshaves, sugar, cotton reels, and stirrup leathers, to frying pans, calico, and fireworks. His brother's Sydney supplier often let him down: 'The X cut saws I ordered were mistaken for pit saws which I have got.'

Much of his trade in goods was as advance payment to the 700-odd Maori workers who supplied him with spars and squared timber. Some commentators have seen this long-standing Hokianga practice as a way of forcing Maori to work year-round, but this would seem to ignore the control the chiefs of the time exerted over their people and the continuing dependence of Pakeha traders on their good will. Although by 1861 trading muskets and powder with Maori had been prohibited because of the Northern War fought between Maori and the government (see Chapter 6, Prestige, power, and politics), relationships between Maori and Pakeha in the Hokianga continued to operate for mutual benefit. Webster relied on 'principal men', such as Wi Tana Papahia and the aging Tamati Waka Nene, to ensure the flow of timber. He often noted (and accepted) that his Maori workers were absent cultivating their crops. He was constantly anxious about the need to reduce his own debts (having himself bought the trade goods on account):

> *Our prospects for the year [1862] are not easily defined, first a great increase in debts last year offset by timber now squared & awaiting a fresh, 2ndly a large tribe out of work having just finished Kaukiro Block & Burdekins land expected by them not available these in debt also, 3rdly natives at the heads in debt & scattered about idle — 4th natives at the head of the river intending to work extensively when their winter crops are planted . . .*

By 1862, Webster was having to look further afield for suitable timber: 'Every year the difficulty attending getting a supply of kauri timber increases.' Although his Maori workers shifted their efforts to more distant inland areas where kauri was still 'handy to watercourses' and 'the work comparatively more easy and speedy', the squared logs had to be retrieved from 'creeks very distant . . . from Kohukohu'. In July, despite 'the natives all [being] at work', the abundant timber, and the ease of getting it down the river ('the floods bring it to the salt water about 3 freshets accomplish this'), he was becoming concerned about the viability of the operation:

My workers are now within a few miles of Kiri Kiri [Kerikeri, Bay of Islands], beyond the line of the Waimate. It takes three days for them to pole their canoes up & as they have to make flat canoes on purpose to convey their food you may imagine the disadvantages under which they work. . . . I question if it would be good policy again to give much credit. I am afraid the natives will find the work now too much for them & lose heart.

Although Webster continued to trade in timber at Kohukohu until his retirement to Opononi in 1874, the easily extractable kauri in the Hokianga was now cut out. The first boom was over. Many of the Pakeha sawmillers who had bought kauri timber land in the Hokianga exchanged their milled blocks for government scrip, using it to take up town sections in Auckland. With the decline of the timber trade, many of the Hokianga Maori, including Nene's people, were left heavily in debt, unable to cut enough timber to pay off their advances.

In the last quarter of the century, the main focus of the kauri industry turned to the Kaipara. In those years, more timber was shipped out of the Kaipara than from all the other deep-water harbours in the kauri region combined.

Full steam ahead on the Kaipara

Until the development of the large steam-driven sawmills in the mid-1860s, Maori communities in the Kaipara provided most of the labour, as they had done in the Hokianga. But even modest steam-driven mills needed fifteen to thirty men to work them, with an equivalent number in the bush. At the time, newly arriving Pakeha settlers expecting to farm their allocated blocks of land were faced instead with dense uncleared bush. Throughout the north, many settlers found alternative employment in the timber industry until they had earned sufficient to support themselves and their families while clearing their land. Dozens of small communities sprang up around the Kaipara Harbour wherever sawmills were based. Some were Maori communities, but more and more housed newly arrived settlers.

By the late 1870s, the expanded Aratapu sawmill complex (then the largest mill in New Zealand) was employing 150 men, with another 150 bush workers supplying the logs. A typical company town developed around the mill. Known as 'Sawdust City', Aratapu became the main settlement in the Northern Wairoa until supplanted by Dargaville further up the Wairoa River in the early twentieth century. Sporting an active temperance movement, a public hall where church services were held, and a library as well as the inevitable hotels, the town made valiant efforts to counteract the all-pervasive scent of sawdust and the hard-drinking habits of bushmen in town on their rare weekends off. Despite these efforts to

Sawdust City — Aratapu in 1900, its unpaved main street sporting shops, a public hall, a library, and hotels.

achieve sobriety and culture, continuing fluctuations in mill ownership and fortunes saw jobs disappear and the town's labour force with them. After temporary closures during a major recession in the 1880s, the mill closed for good in 1906. Aratapu lost its wharfs and its mill buildings, eventually becoming a quiet backwater — the fate of many mill towns.

Felling the forests, clearing the land

At the same time that kauri was being felled for timber, the purchase of large blocks of Maori land for farms and settlement was gathering pace in the north. Kaipara chiefs willingly sold such land in the interests of encouraging Pakeha settlement and the advantages it brought (see also Chapter 6, Prestige, power, and politics). Often heavily forested, land purchased by the Provincial Government from Nga Puhi and Ngati Whatua chiefs, tellingly classed as 'wasteland', was offered as free grants under the 'forty-acre system' between 1858 and 1870. All prospective British settlers over the age of eighteen who could pay their own passage were entitled to these grants, the land becoming freehold after being occupied for five years.

Some areas were set aside for special settlement schemes. Of these, the 1861–1863 Albertland Special Settlement for Baptist non-conformists in the northern Kaipara was

From the coast of Northland to the coast of Southland, lighthouses built from kauri timber shed light on the sea from the late nineteenth century into the twentieth. Twin lighthouses, this one near Pouto on the Kaipara Harbour (photographed in 1940) and the other at Waipapa Point, Southland, were both built in 1883 — to the same design and the same plans. The Waipapa light shone first, on 1 January 1884, followed by the Kaipara light on 1 December 1884.

the most important. After tortuous journeys from Auckland that involved roadless wet bush and precarious canoe voyages across the harbour, the hapless Albertlanders arrived to find their expected townships non-existent and their land still unsurveyed and covered in dense forest.

For all settlers arriving in the north, such forest was seen as an impediment to farming. Clearing the land was an imperative. Although some settlers logged their kauri stands or sold the cutting rights to a contractor, many just felled and burnt the bush. The vast forest seemed inexhaustible — wasting fine timber was not considered reprehensible, merely pragmatic. This approach was encouraged by a Provincial Government hungry for rapid settlement, itself leasing or selling off kauri forests to bush contractors for absurdly low prices to hasten land clearance for farming.

Many of the settlers lured onto blocks of undeveloped land were forced to work in the bush or mills, leaving their women behind to farm rough-cleared land at subsistence level. Dependent on shipping for supplies and access to their isolated farm blocks, many families abandoned their land for life in Auckland, disillusioned by the harsh reality of this promised colonial paradise. Some persisted, gradually clearing the bush and adding to their holdings as adjacent blocks became available. These stalwarts were eventually rewarded, becoming successful dairy farmers when the bush and mill work dried up after the turn of the century.

The Webers from Hanover were typical of the families who persevered in the Kaipara. One of the German families who responded to Premier Vogel's immigration drive in the

Clearing their blocks of land of forest was a priority for arriving settlers. This typical scene photographed in North Auckland in 1902 shows a hard-won clearing with its basic house and outbuildings against the burnt margins of kauri forest.

1870s (German migrants made up about two percent of the population in 1881), the Webers landed in Dunedin in 1878. Frederick and Malvina Weber and their large family soon moved north looking for better prospects, and eventually opted for the Kaipara. Frederick drew 160 hectares on a 999-year lease at Hukatere in a land settlement ballot in 1890. Like most settlers, Frederick and his sons took on whatever work they could find. A skilled architect and lithographer, Frederick worked for the Lands and Survey Department and drew up plans for the Otamatea County Council buildings. He also built butter factories, such as the one on Whakapirau wharf, which used twelve-metre lengths of heart kauri from Chadwick's mill. At the same time he cleared his land and converted it to rough pasture, later adding other blocks of land.

Grandson Edsel Weber, now retired at Matakohe, takes up the family story:

> *The older sons built the family house, right on the water. Later, my father Bruno used to get reject kauri timber from the mill at Pahi to build sheds. He was the youngest of sixteen, and they all lived in the original family house. All the*

brothers worked in the timber trade, felling bush and milling. The older brothers Arnold, Harry, and Ben went to San Francisco after the 1906 earthquake to help rebuild the city.

Bruno built houses through the Depression, bricklaying, plumbing — the lot. And he had a dairy farm, hedged with hawthorn, milking fifty-six cows by hand. At one stage he bought a 'break down' mill — that's part of the display there in the [Otamatea Kauri] Museum — and over-cut a piece of previously milled bush, cutting two-metre lengths of timber from stumps, a lot of it mottled kauri. But he nearly went broke as he couldn't sell the timber.

Descendants of the Weber family still live in the Kaipara, and several generations of Weber men feature as models in the displays at the Otamatea Kauri Museum at Matakohe.

Sailing ships and shipbuilders

The demand for timber accelerated in the mid-nineteenth century as colonial settlement continued and gold rushes took hold on the Coromandel and in the South Island as well as in Australia and North America. Visiting ships were supplemented by locally built vessels. Between 1853 and 1872 alone, shipbuilders in the northern region launched nearly 500 sailing ships for the coastal and overseas timber trade. Most of these ships were built from kauri.

The launching of the first sailing ship built from kauri, the schooner *Herald*, at Paihia, Bay of Islands, in 1826.

The superiority of kauri for shipbuilding had been recognised from the beginning of Pakeha settlement in the north. In 1826, the first sea-going kauri ship — the sixty-tonne schooner *Herald* — was built in the Bay of Islands by Henry Williams and Gilbert Mair for Samuel Marsden. She was soon followed by the larger *Enterprise*, *New Zealander*, and *Sir George Murray*, all built at Horeke in the late 1820s. Both the *Enterprise* and the *Herald* were wrecked on the Hokianga bar within three weeks of each other in 1828 — their short lives a common fate for ships plying the New Zealand coast. In 1848, the largest sailing ship ever built in New Zealand — the 400-tonne three-masted barque *Sterlingshire* — was launched from Nagle Cove, Port Abercrombie (Great Barrier Island). She was probably the first kauri-built ship to reach the London docks.

Although shipbuilding yards of high repute could be claimed by all the deep-water harbours of the north, James Barbour's yard next to the sawmill at Aratapu produced some of the most elegant kauri ships ever built. Of these, the topsail schooner *Huia* was one of the fastest and most famous. During more than fifty years at sea, *Huia* made record passages across the Tasman and from the Kaipara to Lyttelton. Barbour selected the kauri tree for her keel himself from the forest at Kaihu, north of Dargaville. The 33.5-metre-long log was carried by rail to Aratapu for pit-sawing — the longest log ever carried by rail. All *Huia*'s timbers were kauri apart from the framing, which was puriri. The keel, keelson, and external planking were all pit-sawn. Only her inner skin was made from milled kauri planking.

Barbour was a craftsman of considerable skill, with a keen eye for timber and the lines of a ship. Although he could not read or write, he had his own system for calculating tonnage and sail areas for the ships he designed and built. Once he had designed a ship (probably in the traditional way of marking out the half frame on the floor of his shed), he made up bolted wooden moulds in the shapes needed for each piece of framing. Armed with these, Barbour would go into the bush and select matching puriri 'crooks' or 'naturals', then adze them down to their final shapes.

The crooked-growing pohutukawa was also favoured for framing, and many kauri ships had pohutukawa frames. As long as pohutukawa was cut in winter when the wood was low in sap, the frames would last the life of the ship — summer-cut pohutukawa rotted after about five years and contributed to the loss of many otherwise sound ships.

After the First World War, timber production around the Kaipara steadily declined. By the 1920s, fewer than fifty ships per year were using the harbour and the main emphasis of the timber trade and shipbuilding had shifted to Auckland. Much of the New Zealand coastal trade was taken over by robust flat-bottomed scows designed for shallow coastal waters and tidal inlets. Mostly working out of Auckland, the scows carried logs long distances from the outlying kauri districts to the city's waterfront mills, becoming an integral part of the Auckland scene in the early twentieth century.

Launched in 1894, the famous topsail schooner *Huia* built by Barbour sailed on the timber routes for many years. Sold to the Nobel Explosives Company of Glasgow in 1912, she carried explosives across the Tasman until 1950. After then being sold to the Huia Trading Company, she was finally wrecked on a reef near Noumea, New Caledonia, in 1951.

A Swedish-born and Finnish-educated ship's carpenter, Erick Thompson specialised in small boats at the Aratapu yard he established in 1870. His kauri whaleboats were used on Scott's Antarctic expeditions. Many of the flat-bottomed Kaipara punts built to suit the tidal waters of the harbour came from his yard. These punts were sailed or rowed, and could be rowed on mud as well as water. Edsel Weber of Matakohe reminisces:

> *My father Bruno Weber and his sister Martha were both champion rowers and raced Kaipara punts on the harbour in the early 1900s. Martha could out-row many men, and Bruno was tireless — he could row thirty to forty miles before lunch, and another thirty or so afterwards.*

WORKING THE KAIPARA WATERWAYS

Even in the twentieth century, most kauri logs reached the mills and loading wharfs in the Kaipara via the waterways that fed into the harbour. In the 100 years from 1840 to 1940, millions of kauri trees were felled in more than a million hectares of kauri forest surrounding the Kaipara Harbour. Kauri logs accumulated in the creeks for months — and sometimes years — until freshes or floods (often enhanced by simple dams that stored then released the water) sent them on their way to the tidal inlets of the Kaipara. These water-borne journeys of up to 100 kilometres could take weeks.

The Kaipara Harbour

The largest harbour in the Southern Hemisphere, with over 3000 kilometres of coastline, the Kaipara is fed by five major river systems that drain two-thirds of Northland. From smallest creek to major river, all these waterways were used in the extraction of kauri.

Prime Cooper (Ngati Hine) outlines the route taken by some of the logs felled in his home district of Pipiwai (inland Bay of Islands) before the Second World War:

> *Kauri logged on the western side of the Motatau watershed were hauled by bullocks to the Kaikou River, then floated down first to the Mangakahia, then the Wairua, and finally into the Wairoa, where they were stockpiled in the booms for towing to the timber mills at Dargaville. I remember seeing large kauri logs jammed at the top of the falls in the Northern Wairoa. They stayed there through the war before they were released.*

Although in later years, use of waterways and driving dams became increasingly sophisticated (see Chapter 8, Driving forces), the sequence shown by the photographs that follow, mostly taken around the late nineteenth and early twentieth centuries in the Kaipara, is representative of the entire period of kauri extraction.

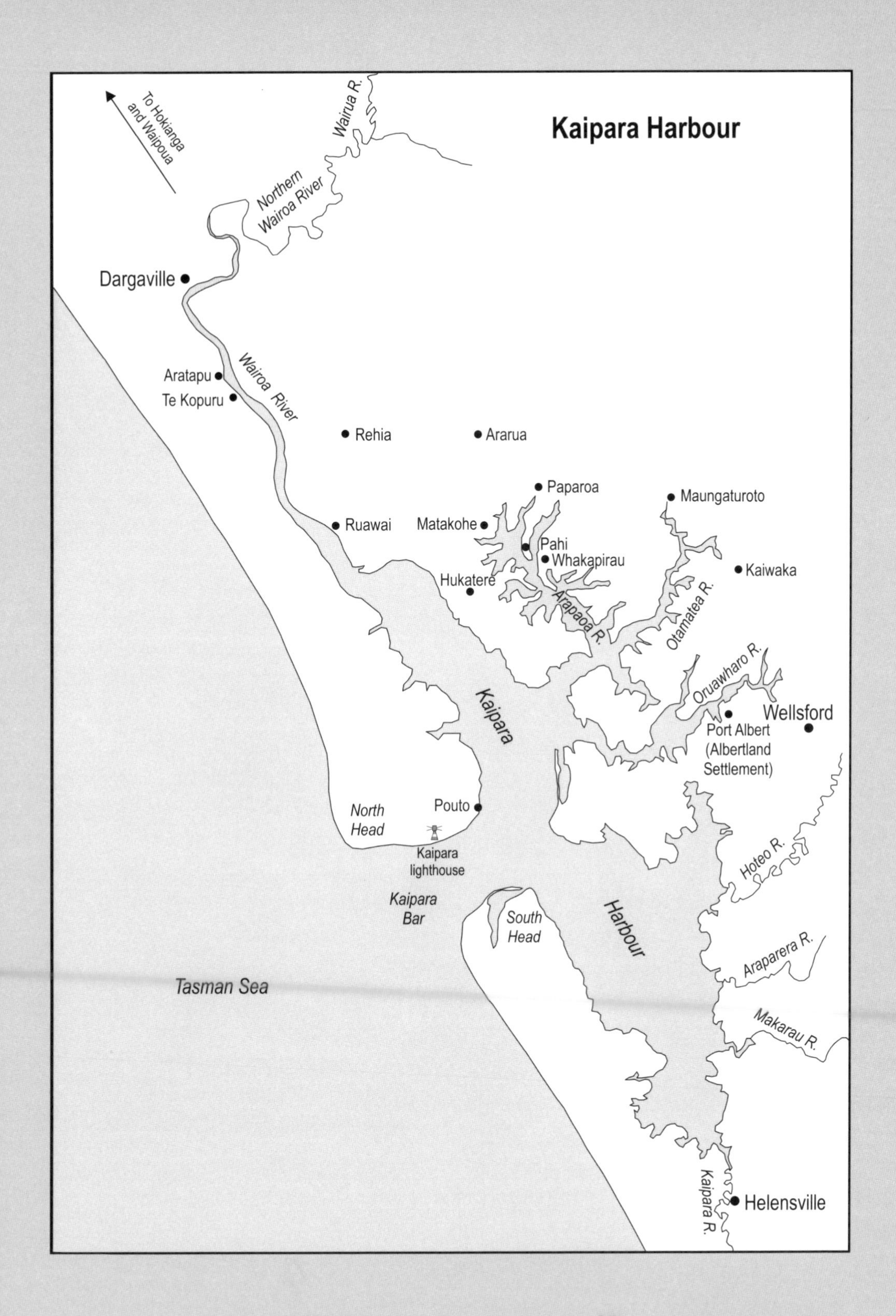
Kaipara Harbour
To Hokianga and Waipoua
Wairua R.
Northern Wairoa River
Dargaville
Wairoa River
Aratapu
Te Kopuru
Rehia
Ararua
Paparoa
Maungaturoto
Ruawai
Matakohe
Pahi
Whakapirau
Kaiwaka
Hukatere
Arapaoa R.
Otamatea R.
Oruawharo R.
Wellsford
Port Albert (Albertland Settlement)
Kaipara
Pouto
North Head
Kaipara lighthouse
Kaipara Bar
South Head
Harbour
Hoteo R.
Araparera R.
Makarau R.
Tasman Sea
Kaipara R.
Helensville

Tree fellers planned the direction of fall so that the tree ended up lying as close as possible to the nearest creek. This kauri was being cut in the Forty-acre Bush, Ararua (Kaipara).

After trimming the head off the tree, these cross-cutters are sawing a fine log into manageable lengths. This tree was being salvaged from Puhipuhi Forest in 1902 after disastrous fires in 1881 and 1887 destroyed close to 1.5 million cubic metres of first-rate kauri timber. Managing a three-metre-long saw could take four men, two on tail ropes. A tall tail-roping tale was recorded in the early 1940s by ninety-three-year-old bushman Charlie Hovell, about his first bush job on the Coromandel in the 1870s:

> *I was tail-roping for Boxer Heath, and we fell a big kauri from the side of the hill. It were about eight foot [2.4 metres] through. We had a stage . . . on the low hill side and we cut down [into the log] about four feet, then we started to lower the stage. Boxer out his head round behind and I said, 'What are you looking for?' He says, 'Are you there?' Well, that hurt me because I'd been pulling my inside out on the tail rope and he'd only been steadying the saw. We lowered our stage and barked our log again, and we got down another two or three feet, and we were going to lower our stage again. Boxer out his head around again. Well, I was waiting for him — we were about twelve feet up on two bungers [punga or treefern logs used as jigger boards] — soon as he out his head I hit him fair in the ear and down the gully he went head over heels.*
>
> (Charlie Hovell, Sound Archives/Nga Taonga Korero)

Using block and tackle, these loggers are hauling large sections of cross-cut kauri out of a gully. The severed head with its massive amount of timber would be left to rot.

Using levers and timber jacks, jackers at Rehia (Northern Wairoa) in 1902 manipulate these logs into position for loading onto a catamaran (timber sledge). Fleets of up to 100 aligned logs were often sequentially jacked long distances on what were known as 'rolling roads'.

A bullock driver and his offsider lead a typical team with eight pairs of yoked bullocks. At the back of the log, a brakeman is poised to wrap a wire rope around a handy tree to control the speed on steep sections.

Once the logs reached the nearest creek, they were jacked into the water and fastened together in a raft for towing downstream. This is Paparoa Creek in 1930, where contractor Bob McAdam was transporting kauri logs for processing at West's mill at Helensville.

Griff Griffin recounts an epic rafting journey in the early 1900s:

> *The logs . . . formed a fleet many chains in length, and in many places eight or ten deep. When the winter floods came, twenty or thirty men were engaged in loosening the huge piles of logs, and starting them on their way . . . to the tidal water booms on the Northern Wairoa River, some seventy miles down stream. [The three most experienced men accompanied the raft of logs, using] a twelve-foot flat-bottomed punt . . . to carry tools, tucker, swags, and two heavy waterproof canvas sheets — one to sleep on, the other for a shelter at night. . . . Rain began to fall heavily on the fifth day out, and continued for two days without ceasing. The stream overflowed . . . taking hundreds of logs off course. The towing and manoeuvring of these logs, getting them back into the current, took many extra days, as a consequence of which our tucker dwindled and finally petered out. . . . After three days and two nights of cold and wet clothing, without a bite to eat, the outlook was grim.*
>
> (Reed 1964)

After hearing a rooster crow in the early hours in what they had thought was uninhabited dense bush, the three 'gaunt, bearded, and soaking-wet bushmen' floundered through dense undergrowth in breast-high floodwater to trace the rooster and the welcome respite of a remote farmhouse.

At the end of a long journey down the Wairoa River, a raft of kauri logs arrives at the Aratapu mill in 1902, where it lies alongside stockpiled already-sawn logs waiting to be shipped out of the Kaipara.

Percy Eaddy describes crossing the treacherous Kaipara bar with a load of logs on the scow *Hawk*:

> *We saw a great Pacific greybeard gradually rise and tower in all his majesty right in our track. . . . On and inward it swept, irresistible and awe-inspiring, till suddenly the great crest of it began to curl, and just as we were about to rise and let it pass underneath our hull, the whole length of it, for half-a-mile on either side of us, toppled forward in a seething mass of white foam.*
>
> *For a few moments the* Hawk *seemed to be on the point of annihilation. Her hull, deckload and everything below the great straining [sail] booms, were completely submerged in a welter of boiling foam, but, shaking herself clear, like a great Newfoundland dog after a dip, she shot through it and surged onwards ready for the next encounter.*
>
> *We repeated the performance once or twice in lesser degree as we worked seawards and as the final breaker passed in under our lee we heaved a sigh of relief to be quit of the dread Kaipara Bar . . .*
>
> (Eaddy 1936)

CHAPTER 6

Capitalising on kauri

COLONIAL POLITICS, AUCKLAND, AND THE KAURI TRADE, 1840s–1920s

Changing places

In the middle of Auckland's Commercial Bay, coastal schooners nudge the wharf, side by side like suckling piglets. The Governor Wynyard, *tall smoke stack pluming proudly, trundles homewards across the harbour, returning from Otahuhu on its regular run. Across the bay, a brig loads sawn kauri timber for Sydney. Behind the bay, small wooden cottages jostle each other amidst grander tall buildings along the laid-out lines of unpaved clay roads. Beyond the point at Freeman's Bay, sawmills and brickworks bustle with the business of building a city. It is 1852. Already boasting close to 6000 residents, Auckland City — capital of the newest British colony and the largest settlement in the country — is immersed in commercial enterprise and colonial politics.*

> *The Waitemata is well adapted for boat-sailing. Canoes from all parts of the Gulf are continually arriving and departing; and with nearly 100 vessels from distant ports, upwards of 600 coasters, and nearly 2,000 canoes yearly entering the port, its sheltered waters present a lively, business-like appearance.*
>
> (WILLIAM SWAINSON 1853)

An 1852 Auckland scene, looking west from Fort Britomart past the Gore Street jetty in Commercial Bay, along Fort Street on the foreshore to the Queen Street wharf (right middle distance), Smales Point (right), and the Wesleyan Chapel (left). Old St Matthews Church can be seen left and St Patricks Cathedral centre background. The paddle steamer *Governor Wynyard* appears in the foreground.

Now a decade beyond its founding on the shores of the Waitemata Harbour, the colonial capital had resolutely turned its back on a shaky and debt-ridden beginning. Its presence owed more to pressure from northern Maori chiefs, Pakeha traders, CMS missionaries, and advocates of immigration than it owed to any British aspirations to make New Zealand a formal colony.

Tricks or treaties

By the late 1830s, local chiefs were asking for the appointment of a Governor to take control of the increasing numbers of Pakeha in the Bay of Islands and the Hokianga. In turn, established Pakeha traders and missionaries were also seeking some form of higher authority to keep uppity chiefs in check. Missionaries and advocates of what would become the New Zealand Company were complaining to the British Government about the dangers of insidious settlement by over-stayers from whaling ships and ex-convicts from Australia — these 'undesirable' settlers were undermining New Zealand's appeal to more genteel immigrants. A reluctant British Government appointed William Hobson as

James Busby served as British Resident in the Bay of Islands between 1833 and early 1840.

Captain William Hobson, appointed as first Lieutenant-Governor of New Zealand in 1839, served until his death in 1842.

Lieutenant-Governor in 1839, then proclaimed British sovereignty over New Zealand with the signing of the Treaty of Waitangi on 6 February 1840.

Only five years earlier, the British Resident James Busby (appointed to the Bay of Islands in 1833 to help regulate dealings between Pakeha and Maori) had twice formally acknowledged the sovereignty of the northern Maori chiefs. His motivation had been both practical and political.

By the early 1830s, practical problems of ship registration were besetting the fledgling Hokianga kauri timber trade. Although the Governor of New South Wales had issued licences for the kauri ships built at Horeke, some had experienced being temporarily seized by Sydney Customs in apparent breaches of the terms — perhaps first examples of underhand Trans-Tasman trickery. With Maori and Pakeha traders equally anxious to avoid further repeats, Busby asked the leading chiefs in the Bay of Islands and the Hokianga to select a national flag for a New Zealand shipping register. This was to be established under their authority and counter-signed by him as British Resident. The status and significance of such a flag were well understood by the chiefs, who had taken to flying symbols of their authority soon after the earliest visits of flag-bedecked ships. At Waitangi in March 1834,

The national flag flies at Waitangi. One of three designed by Busby, this flag was selected by the northern Maori chiefs in 1834 to establish a New Zealand shipping register.

thirty chiefs with due and solemn ceremony voted on three flags. Their choice was raised with the Union Jack to the triumphant firing of a twenty-one gun naval salute.

After the exploratory voyages of Surville and Marion du Fresne in the late eighteenth century, the French had continued to show an interest in New Zealand, with obvious political implications. Awareness of the French presence pushed Busby towards his second acknowledgement of chiefly authority. Eventually, alarmed by the eccentric Baron de Thierry's intentions to set himself up as an independent potentate in the Hokianga, Busby initiated the Declaration of Independence of New Zealand — without prior approval of the British Government. In this 1835 Declaration, the chiefs of the 'Confederation of United Tribes' (formed for the purpose) stated their independence, claimed sovereign rights over northern New Zealand, and requested protection of these rights from King William IV. Busby's sleight of hand reaffirmed official recognition of chiefly authority — at least in the minds of the chiefs.

No wonder then that the reversal of that recognition implicit in English-language but not Maori-language versions of the 1840 Treaty of Waitangi caused trouble once the new colonial authorities tried to challenge Maori authority. That challenge continues to cause trouble today.

Prestige, power, and politics

As the number of Pakeha settlers increased in the years immediately after the Treaty, the chiefs competed for control of the new towns springing up on the blocks of land they sold to the colonial authorities for that purpose — a familiar pattern on a larger scale. But when the colonial authorities sought to impose rules and regulations on Maori as well as the new Pakeha settlers, discontent set in among disillusioned chiefs.

In the north, Maori reactions depended on perceptions of the value of Pakeha settlement and the degree to which chiefs were willing to sell land to the government agents. The Nga Puhi chiefs saw their prestige and power challenged when the colonial capital moved in 1840 from Kororareka (now Russell) in the overcrowded Bay of Islands to the

Nga Puhi chief Tamati Waka Nene, intermediary and peacemaker between Hone Heke and Governors FitzRoy and Grey during the Northern War in the mid-1840s.

Nga Puhi chief Hone Heke is flanked by his wife Hariata (left) and his uncle and Ngati Hine ally Kawiti in this watercolour painted in 1846.

conveniently under-populated Tamaki Isthmus. It would not have helped that moving the capital south was partly at the invitation of Te Kawau, a chief of Ngati Whatua, a tribe who had only recently returned to their lands at Tamaki — abandoned after their defeat by Nga Puhi in the Musket Wars. At the same time, the Nga Puhi chiefs saw their prosperity challenged by the government's attempts to capture some of their revenue by the imposition of customs duties, land-sale taxes, and attempted restrictions on the felling of kauri — now a major source of their economic wealth. Angered, Tamati Waka Nene of the Hokianga (without whose support the Treaty would never have been signed) threatened to chop down a kauri at the Governor's feet if he dared set either foot in the Hokianga.

Hone Heke, a northern Nga Puhi chief and nephew of the famous Hongi Hika, and his new ally from the southern Bay of Islands, Kawiti (Ngati Hine), went further. Vociferous opponents of the sales of land, they chose to attack that veritable symbol of sovereignty, the Union Jack — which now flew without its chief-chosen companion flag at Kororareka. In 1844, Heke chopped down the kauri flagstaff and then its three successive replacements over the next two years.

The subtlety of this symbolic gesture was lost on Governor FitzRoy and the colonists.

Robert FitzRoy, Governor of New Zealand 1843–1845.

Sir George Grey, Governor of New Zealand 1845–1853 and 1861–1868, then elected Premier 1877–1879.

Nene, although sympathetic to Heke's cause, undertook to protect the replacement flagstaffs for the Governor. His diplomacy gained the removal of the duties and taxes in return. But Heke's sacking and inadvertent burning of Kororareka in 1845 after he had felled the fourth flagstaff (and things got out of hand) went too far. Nene saw this as an attack on his own mana — he had personally seen to its reinstallation. He engaged Heke in low-level skirmishes in which some Pakeha became involved, among them Webster and Maning (see Chapter 5, Energy and enterprise on the Hokianga). An alarmed FitzRoy called in troops from New South Wales. Their arrival saw the onset of the Northern War, 'Heke's War', in which for the first time Maori fought for the government against kin.

The outcome of the fighting was inconclusive. Neither the numerically superior and well-equipped British troops nor the defiant Heke and Kawiti — besieged in their innovative earth bunkers at a series of pa in the inland Bay of Islands — were able to force a final victory. The peace brokered by Nene in 1846 with FitzRoy's replacement Governor Grey acknowledged both Maori mana and Pakeha power. Grey claimed victory, but Heke and Kawiti retained their land and continued to flaunt their independence. Nene was rewarded for his support, becoming an acknowledged advisor to the colonial authorities. A similar role was taken up by other notable chiefs living in and near Auckland, among them Patuone (Nga Puhi), Tuhaere (Ngati Whatua), and Te Wherowhero (Waikato).

For some decades to come, the chiefs retained considerable autonomy and prestige in places where Maori and Pakeha interacted on equal terms. They held total autonomy in places isolated from Pakeha influence. But in places where large blocks of land changed hands under Governor Grey and the number of Pakeha steadily increased, the real power began to shift from the marae of the Maori chiefs to the new buildings of the provincial governors.

From enterprise to elegance

In the years of peace that followed the end of the Northern War in 1846, colonial Auckland began to flourish. By the early 1850s, three-fifths of the whole population of New Zealand (Maori and Pakeha) lived in Auckland Province. Unlike the five organised settlements of Wakefield's New Zealand Company, with their carefully controlled mix of suitable settlers, the Pakeha attracted to Auckland were self-selected and self-made. Already established merchants and land speculators, colonial officials, and military officers were boosted by soldier pensioners and arriving settlers (mostly from Australia). Optimistic and opportunistic, Auckland citizens set about making capital out of commerce and colonisation.

Commerce in Auckland Province was firmly focused on trade and the extraction industries — kauri timber and gum, later boosted by Coromandel gold. At first, in the 1850s and 1860s, Maori traders dominated, arriving by canoes and small coasters from the Bay of Islands, the Hauraki Gulf, and the Waikato to sell produce from their now-extensive agricultural enterprises. Maori supplied food, firewood, and building timber, both for Auckland's use and for export. Quick to learn new techniques, Maori tradesmen also helped build the housing and public works needed for the rapidly growing city.

In the 1860s, well over a decade after the Northern War, Governor Grey again went to war with Maori tribes. His pretext was a perceived threat from the Maori unity signalled by emerging groups such as the King movement in the Waikato, the organised resistance against land selling in Taranaki, and a number of prophetic movements in the Hokianga, Wanganui, and elsewhere. The New Zealand Wars saw the arrival of thousands of soldiers to inflate the Pakeha population and economy of Auckland. Wartime Auckland boomed.

Sitting at the hub of kauri country with sea access in all directions, Auckland sawmillers and timber merchants were ideally placed to take advantage of expanding domestic and export markets. Kauri provided the best and cheapest raw material available for building the new colony. From the Far North to the distant south of the South Island, kauri timber was used for everything — farmers' houses and city mansions, civic and commercial buildings, railway sleepers and bridges, sailing ships and luxury yachts, butter churns and barrels (kauri is non-tainting), fine furniture, and split-paling fences.

The seat of government moved again in 1865, from Auckland to Wellington. At the same time, the military withdrew and Auckland's prosperity slumped. The four main Auckland timber merchants bought up many of the region's faltering sawmills and their kauri forest blocks, often using borrowed money. When recession again hit hard in the mid-1880s, many kauri timber mills were taken over by the Melbourne-based Kauri Timber Company, formed for the purpose in 1889. Production of kauri timber picked up again later, hitting its peak in 1906 with over 3500 people employed at mills throughout Auckland Province and over 440,000 cubic metres of timber being cut. Although huge amounts of kauri were being used in New Zealand at that time, kauri timber was also one of the country's biggest exports.

Serviced solely from the sea until the early twentieth century (rail links from Auckland did not reach Wellington until about 1910), Auckland's fluctuating market-driven fortunes depended on a growing fleet of ships. From the cutters, schooners, and flat-bottomed scows involved in the coastal trade, to the sailing ships and steamers involved in the export trade, many of these ships were built locally from kauri.

Up the creek

In the mid-1840s, small craft were already being built for Maori skippers and owners taking advantage of the growing Pakeha population of Auckland and its demands. Most of these craft were built from kauri, many of them by Maori who had been trained at the first Pakeha shipbuilding yards. By the 1850s, over 100 Maori-owned cutters and

Following in the footsteps of their famous father Robert Logan, the Logan brothers continued to build elegant prize-winning kauri-hulled racing yachts until about 1910, classic yachts that dominated the highly competitive Auckland sailing regattas well into the twentieth century.

Flat-bottomed scows dominated the coastal timber trade from the early 1870s. The scow *Rangi* is seen here a long way up a creek, waiting for the tide.

schooners were plying eastern coastal waters from the Bay of Plenty to the Far North. Until the late 1860s, Maori dominated local shipping in the same way that they dominated agriculture. Many of these small coastal craft carried loads of pit-sawn kauri timber to Auckland among their varied cargoes.

When large-scale production of squared logs started in the mid-1860s, steam-driven mills sprang up along the many tidal creeks and harbours of the northern region (see Chapter 5, Full steam ahead on the Kaipara). Shallow-drafted, flat-bottomed craft were designed in the early 1870s that could fetch up alongside these mills, dispensing with the need for lighters to load ships standing off in deeper water. Based on the timber-carrying barges that serviced the American Great Lakes, the new craft became known as 'scows'. By the end of the century, fleets of these practical craft, mostly rigged as schooners, dominated the coastal kauri trade. Many of them worked out of the Waitemata Harbour, bringing back kauri logs for the growing number of Auckland-based timber mills.

Timber scows were solidly constructed to carry their heavy loads. They were designed without sides above deck so that the logs could be rolled on and off the reinforced deck

WORKHORSES OF THE SEA

Sturdy scows battled gale-force winds and heavy seas, negotiated tidal creeks and treacherous harbour entrances, and survived strandings on exposed beaches. With working lives of more than fifty years, kauri scows became the stuff of legends.

Captured at sea

In 1917, during the First World War, the scow *Moa* was sailing from Tauranga to Auckland when she was boarded by a party of escaped German prisoners. Under the command of the sword-brandishing Count Felix von Luckner, captain of the wrecked German raider *Seeadler*, the prisoners had made a daring escape from Motuihe Island in the Hauraki Gulf on board the commanding officer's own launch *Pearl*. Captain Bourke and the crew of the *Moa* were declared prisoners of the Kaiser by the Count, who hoisted the German ensign on the scow. The crew were forced to jettison part of their cargo of rimu and bear away for the Kermadecs and its store of castaway provisions over 1000 kilometres away (five days' sailing).

Moa's unexpected change of course was spotted by Captain Francis on the scow *Rangi*, a few kilometres ahead and also loaded with rimu for Auckland. Apparently also targeted, the *Rangi* had been sailing too fast for von Luckner to catch her. Aware that the Germans had escaped, Captain Francis put into Port Charles on the Coromandel to raise the alarm. The cable steamer *Iris* gave chase. Catching up with the *Moa* at the Kermadecs, the *Iris* put a shot across her bows with one of two six-pound guns specially fitted for the pursuit. The Count and his party were forced to surrender. The *Moa* returned to Auckland under tow, the resigned Germans under armed guard on board the *Iris*.

Versatile survivors

Skippered by descendants of northern families, two kauri-built scows have traversed the waters of the Hokianga and the Kaipara in recent years, carrying tourists on sight-seeing voyages.

Alma, the last of the large deck scows, was built by well-known shipbuilder George Niccol at Torpedo Bay (Devonport) in 1902. She carried kauri timber, sand, and shingle on the northern coast. Registered as a world heritage ship, she now explores Hokianga history with Graeme Darroch at the helm.

Te Aroha was built on a framework of pohutukawa at Totara North, Whangaroa Harbour in 1909. Most of her kauri planking, keel, keelsons, and stringers all came from the one log. With an insulated hold, she carried frozen meat carcasses from Wairoa to Napier, and later traded across Cook Strait out of Nelson. She clocked up more than 10,000 crossings in her seventy years of toil. The refitted *Te Aroha* first sailed on eco-tourism ventures in the Hauraki Gulf, and has plied the Kaipara with Avin Curel at the helm.

A fleet of timber scows anchored at the Kauri Timber Company boom in Mechanics Bay.

using boiler-driven derricks and parbuckling chains. Up to twenty-five metres long, most scows had strong bolted kauri frames. Their heavy kauri planking was sheathed to the waterline with totara as a protection against toredo worm. A closed-off hold a metre deep served only as buoyancy space, with the logs all carried on the deck:

> *It was a most fascinating sight to watch a long scow come in and discharge her cargo of great kauri logs. In she would sweep, resembling at a distance a huge piled-up raft of logs, urged along by a great press of sail.*
>
> (Eaddy 1936)

Scows carried logs to Auckland from throughout the kauri region, from Katikati in the southernmost area of kauri forest, the Coromandel and western Hauraki, and from the Waitakere Ranges and the Kaipara. Kauri from the Waitakere Ranges was transported to Whatipu in the Manukau Harbour, some being shipped directly overseas from there. Even after steam tugs and rafting became the main means of transporting logs to Auckland from distant mill sites, the scows continued in service, being able to carry sawn timber and 'sinkers' (logs that had no buoyancy) as well as logs.

Long after the logging days were over, engine-powered scows continued to ply New Zealand's coastal waters, carrying bulk loads of coal, shingle, and cement well beyond the middle of the twentieth century (see this chapter, Workhorses of the sea).

Going to San Francisco

Even small sailing ships — owned and crewed by Maori or Pakeha — became involved in the early export trade. In the 1840s, many Northland-built kauri ships took loads of timber to far-flung places like Mauritius (returning with sugar), the Pacific Islands, Australia, China, the American West Coast, and Britain. As well as pit-sawn timber, these ships carried cargoes of Maori-grown potatoes, flour and wheat, butter, salt pork, and beef. By the 1850s, San Francisco was the destination of many of these ships, taking advantage of the opportunity for large profits from the huge demand for food and timber generated by the California gold rushes.

As early as 1849, the enterprising Macky brothers shipped twenty prefabricated kauri houses from Auckland to San Francisco, to find they had been pipped at the post by timber traders from the Eastern States. The houses all sold, but they recovered the cost of only three of them. Other early voyages to San Francisco were made by the brig *Kiwi* (built on the Northern Wairoa in 1848), also with speculative cargoes that included kauri timber, roofing shingles, and more prefabricated kauri houses. In 1850, John Logan Campbell (accompanied by Hokianga's John Webster) made a good profit in San Francisco from

Maori-grown produce. Many other adventurous traders followed, including Maori, some staying on to try for a fortune on the goldfields.

At that time, the infant California State was easily accessible only by sea. The distance from New Zealand (11,000 kilometres) was less than half the distance of the supply route around the Horn from the American eastern seaboard. As a result, trade between Auckland and San Francisco flourished, then accelerated once gold was also discovered in Australia and then in New Zealand in the 1860s. From 1870, a regular four-weekly mail and passenger steamship service linked Auckland and Sydney to San Francisco. This was the first of a series of inter-colonial steamer services that continued until the early 1900s. By 1897, forty percent of Auckland's kauri timber was being exported to Australia and the California goldfields, providing mining props and shoring timber, railway sleepers, wharfing and bridging, paving slabs, and construction timber for the booming mine settlements and their supporting cities.

In Australia, kauri timber helped build Sydney, where kauri floors can still be found in mid-nineteenth-century houses. It was reported in 1899 that kauri paving slabs were to be used to pave the railway platforms of Melbourne, and tenders were anticipated for kauri street paving for both cities. In California, kauri timber helped build San Francisco as the population grew from 500 to 250,000 between 1850 and 1880, and again after the disastrous earthquake and fire of 1906. Many of the warehouses rebuilt on the San Francisco waterfront still feature kauri beams.

Houses as history

From workers' cottages to mansions, New Zealand's colonial architecture owes much to the history of the kauri trade. The earliest pit-sawn kauri houses in the Bay of Islands and the Hokianga were often built by ships' carpenters and reflected their origins. Styles ranged from traditional English Georgian to those from the whaling seaboard of America and the hotter climates of India and the Caribbean. But by the time Hobson moved his capital from Kororareka to Auckland in 1840, taking the carpenter 'mechanics' with him, the basic square colonial house with its hipped roof and wide verandahs was well established.

Many grander town houses built during the 1840s to 1860s were in the Gothic Revival style. Although English in appearance, these were based on American designs that had adapted European and British brick or stone Gothic styles for construction in timber. Many such houses sported doors and pre-assembled windows imported from America.

After the 1860s, the California connection had a major influence on New Zealand house design. At the same time that the export kauri trade to San Francisco was expanding, the industrial revolution was producing the steam-powered woodworking machinery that enabled the first mass production of timber houses in New Zealand. Kauri provided much of the timber needed for the estimated 30,000 wooden houses built in the 1860s and the 40,000 built in the 1870s. Two-thirds of all houses in the North Island were probably kauri. From Auckland to Otago, such houses were built using new American building techniques and distinctive architectural designs that filtered through to New Zealand via the trading and goldfield links with San Francisco.

With the ease of producing machine-sawn timber, the plain square colonial cottage evolved into the more elaborate Victorian villa, sporting a gabled projection with bay windows that interrupted the line of the old-style verandah across the front of the house. After the 1870s, these single-bay villas became the basic style for ordinary housing. Speculative builders erected suburbs of villas in cities like Auckland, Wellington, and Dunedin to accommodate the growing numbers of immigrants. With conspicuous Italianate features and many variations on the gable-and-bay theme, what became known as the 'bay villa' owed much of its style and appearance to similar villas still lining the streets in the suburbs of San Francisco.

To what extent the nineteenth-century villa of San Francisco itself owed its fabric and façades to imported New Zealand kauri is unknown, as whole blocks of the city were destroyed in the 1906 fire, including over 12,000 wooden houses. But it seems likely that

More than 360 simple pit-sawn kauri cottages like this one (now in the Howick Historical Village) were built in the late 1840s for pensioner soldiers retiring from the Royal New Zealand Fencibles, established to defend Auckland against possible Maori attack.

Above The elegant upright façades of the two-storeyed wooden shops on Shortland Street, photographed some time after 1865, bravely ignore the rough scoria-surfaced street, the open drains, and lack of lighting or water supply of Victorian Auckland, which had much in common with American frontier townscapes of the same vintage.

Right Machine-produced fretwork and decorative items cut from kauri adorned New Zealand houses from the 1880s onwards. This pattern was known as Tylee Lace.

the traffic was two-way — kauri and carpenters going to San Francisco, then bringing American designs back to New Zealand. This traffic continued after the 1906 fire, with New Zealand carpenters like the Weber brothers (see Chapter 5, Felling the forests, clearing the land) crossing the Pacific to help rebuild the devastated city. What is certain is that New Zealand visitors to the villa-lined streets of the Bay suburbs of San Francisco today can have a strong sense of déjà vu.

In the New Zealand of the late nineteenth century, middle-class immigrants flaunted their new wealth by decorating their villas with elaborate fretwork, mouldings, brackets, and scrolls. A huge variety of such features, based on European and English designs, was mass-produced by machinery from the 1880s on. Kauri timber companies in Auckland published catalogues and pattern books from which aspiring villa owners could mix and

The villas of Wright Street, Wellington (above), built in 1905, bear a strong resemblance to similar houses in San Francisco, like these American Queen Anne-style villas in Steiner Street, which date from 1894 (below).

ELEGANCE AND THE ELITE

Kemp House, Kerikeri, Bay of Islands, is New Zealand's oldest surviving timber building. Built in 1821 of pit-sawn kauri, this historic mission house is an example of Georgian vernacular architecture and was similar in style to Samuel Marsden's house at Parramatta outside Sydney.

Built of kauri in 1861, Highwic (Epsom) is a classic example of American Gothic Revival style using vertical boards and battens.

One of the largest wooden buildings in the world, Wellington's 1876 Government Buildings (designed by William Clayton in classical Italianate palazzo style) were built of kauri timber to imitate stone construction.

Antrim House, built of kauri in Wellington in 1904 as a domestic example of grand Italianate style, now houses the New Zealand Historic Places Trust.

match decorative components to dress up the gable-and-bay structure of their new houses. By the turn of the century, many of the patterns offered by companies like the Kauri Timber Company were identical to those offered by their American counterparts.

The production of fully fledged Edwardian 'bay villas' spanned the major years of the kauri industry, reaching its peak in the first decade of the twentieth century. Villa style and decorative detail varied throughout the country according to climate and the influence of individual architects. In Auckland, villa scale and grandeur varied from the elaborate mansions at the top of the street to the simple single-bay houses of the lowly worker at the bottom. But wherever villas were built, whether of kauri or other timbers, many remain today as lasting evidence of the influence on New Zealand's architecture of the kauri trade and its links to California — an influence that continued with the introduction of the California bungalow after the villa went out of fashion in the early twentieth century.

Kitchen sink to kauri sideboard

Colonial carpenters obliged their customers with all interior fittings. The straight grain of kauri and its ease of working made it an ideal timber for lining walls and ceilings, with the joins between the wide planks covered with battens. Many early cottages and churches were lined with dressed vertical kauri boards, usually dark-stained to suit Victorian tastes. Up until the 1920s, bedrooms and kitchens were often treated with narrow tongue-and-groove match lining made from kauri. Essential kitchen fittings such as sink benches and tubs made from kauri were used throughout the country and can still be picked up in demolition yards.

Later, when woodworking machinery made the work easy, interior wood-lined walls were dressed up with timber mouldings like ceiling cornices, architraves, and skirtings. The kauri timber companies produced pattern books for interior as well as exterior decoration. The walls themselves were papered over — the warm glow of kauri wood was not regarded as being elegant enough. Similarly, intricate kauri fireplace surrounds and mantelpieces were given marble finishes, and panelled kauri doors were painted or artificially grained to look like more familiar woods. Magnificent kauri staircases with moulded banisters selected from the pattern books still grace many grand old villas today, their glory revealed once layers of paint are stripped away.

Carpenters and joiners of the day also turned their hands to furniture making, producing simple tables and chairs, dressers and cabinets, bedsteads and wash-stands for the houses they built. As they experimented with local woods to reproduce Victorian designs, they soon found that kauri was the perfect timber for furniture making, as it neither warped nor shrank. Early furniture makers usually disguised its plain grain and honey colour with dark stains and heavy varnishes. Later, as immigrants became more affluent, houses more elaborate, and machinery more sophisticated, skilled cabinet-makers

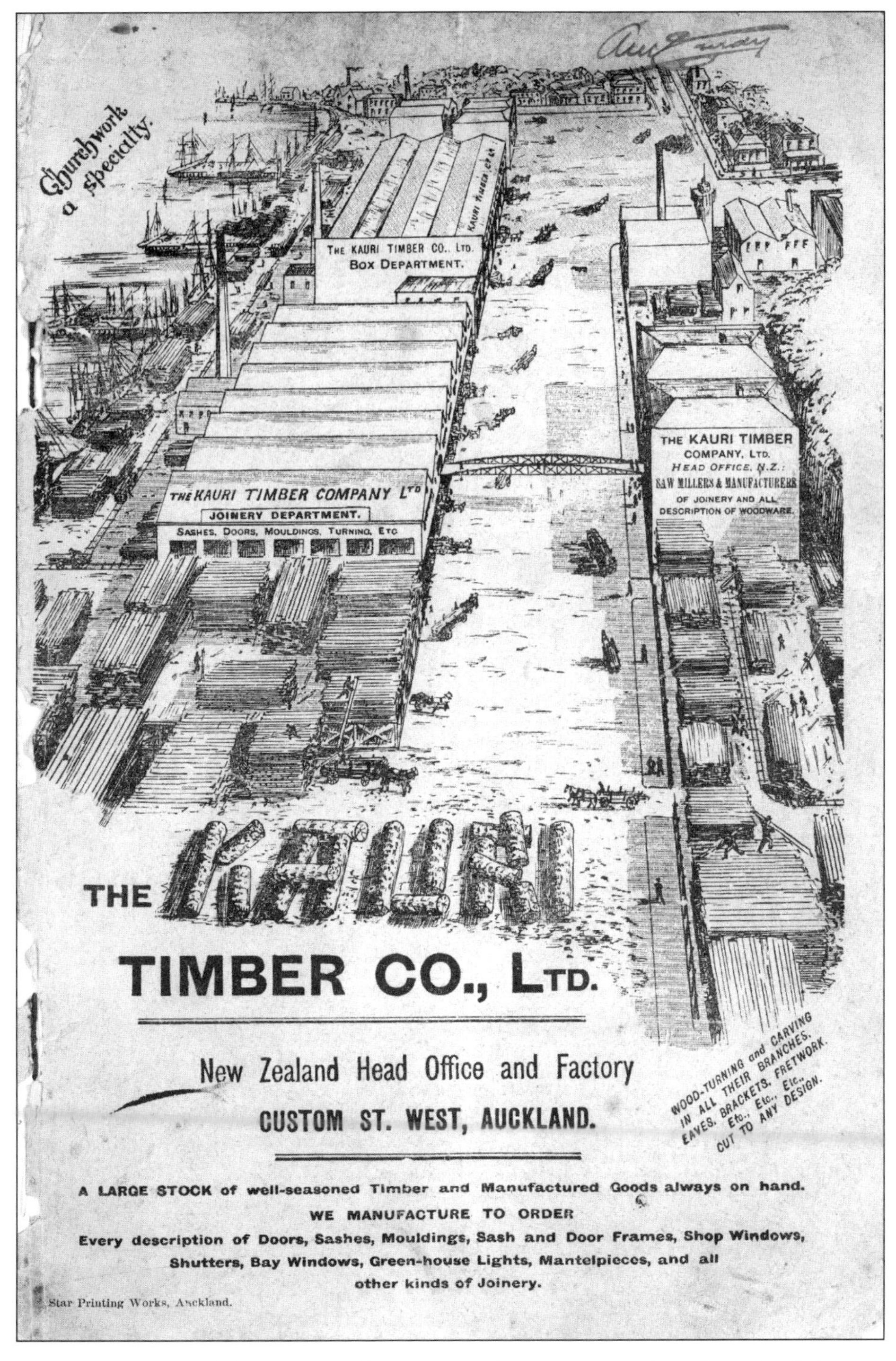

A bird's-eye view of the Kauri Timber Company's premises and loading wharfs in Auckland about 1906, used as the company's catalogue cover.

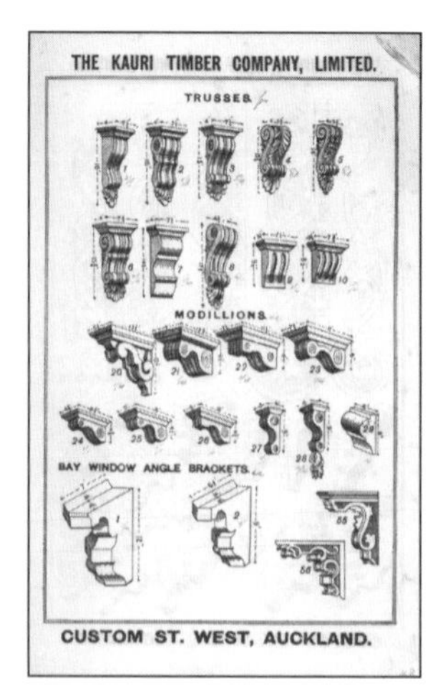

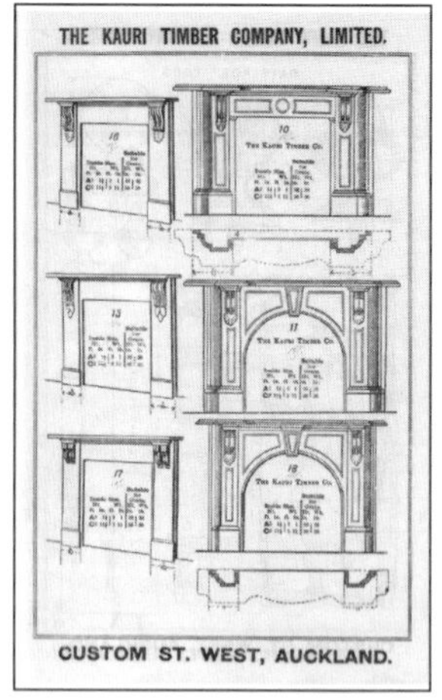

Pages from an early 1900s Kauri Timber Company catalogue illustrate the wide range of patterns available for decorating the exterior and interior of Edwardian bay villas.

were employed by the sash and door companies. The furniture they made showed signs of American influence, both from the pattern books and from mass-produced furniture imported from America. Producing everything from cabinets with simple classical lines to ornate and (to modern eyes) cumbersome wardrobes, many Victorian craftsmen created pieces of superb furniture that are now collectors' items.

The more desirable pieces were often made from rare mottled or figured kauri. No one knows why some kauri produce timber with flecked or dappled grain. Some consider it the result of disease, others the result of pieces of bark being trapped within the growing wood. Growing conditions may be the cause, with trees from rocky terrain more likely to have mottled wood. Regardless of its origin, talented Auckland cabinet-makers like William Norrie and Anton and William Seuffert (who specialised in elegant, intricate inlay work) made the most of mottled kauri, often combining it with other fine native timbers such as totara, rewarewa, and puriri. Rather than develop new designs, the best New Zealand furniture makers took traditional styles and made them their own with the use of native woods and local motifs that reflected the new country in which they found themselves.

Chapter 7

Gum spear, spade, and scraper

LIFE ON THE GUM-FIELDS, 1830s–1930s

Beyond the black stump

Spade, spear, and sugar-bag swag of kauri gum slung across his shoulders, the gum-digger picks his way among stunted tea-tree, fern, ancient stumps, and black water-filled holes towards the dry higher ground. Tucked in a hollow amid sheltering clumps of taller tea-tree, a straggle of tent-like shacks is home until good pickings from the local gum-field run out. The gum-digger dumps his heavy swag or pikau as he calls it (Maori for 'carry on the back') and props his tools against the sod chimney. Inside, he rekindles the fire under a blackened billy of tinned meat stew with the aid of a handful of gum scrapings. Mud-encrusted trousers slung to dry, wet boots shed, he now has time to relax before tackling the evening's work of scraping the dirt and rind from his growing pile of gum. It is day's end in 1895 on the Aupouri Peninsula, the topmost tip of New Zealand. The gum-digger is one of nearly 7000 people working full-time in the gum-fields of Auckland Province.

Lurking beneath the surface of the bleak landscapes of the north, deposits of kauri gum bear witness to the ancient presence of kauri forests (see Chapter 2, Beating a retreat). In these landscapes — whether scrubland and swamp, or newly felled, stump-strewn, and

TOOLS AND TECHNIQUES

In about 1910 a Northland gum-digger returns home laden with his day's booty of gum in a sacking pikau or swag, his gum spear, axe, and reinforced Skelton gum spade on his shoulder. Skelton spades came in different handle lengths and blade sizes, with 'o' being the most popular.

Left An unidentified Maori digs for swamp gum using bucket and Skelton spade, his finds deposited in the woven flax kete beside him.

Below Teams of Dalmatians systematically worked the gum-fields, digging deep trenches that needed continual pumping to remove the water. Early designs adapted from sailing-ship pumps used empty jam tins soldered together into a pipe up to four metres long, with a leather clapper valve at the lower end. Operated by a wooden rod with a T-handle and cone-shaped plunger inserted inside the pipe, a hand-pump could extract as much as eighteen litres of water at each stroke.

Jack Kuljish works a primitive hurdy-gurdy. Using the same principle as a giant flour sifter, a basic drum with a perforated bottom was fitted with a hand-driven revolving shaft and paddle to separate out lumps of gum from shovelfuls of earth, using lots of water. A hand-pump can be seen on the left.

A power-driven gum-washing machine being operated at Ahipara Hill in the late 1920s or early 1930s. Dempsey Hokai (far left in striped shirt), Ivan Yelavich (far right, holding hat), and Allan McPherson with his hand on the wheel.

Regular bleeding of kauri as if they were rubber trees became standard practice. These gum-bleeders are climbing a badly scarred kauri at Herekino. Gum-bleeding was banned after 1905 when the severe damage to the trees and the persistent firing of the forests by gum-bleeders caused concern. But illicit and lucrative gum-bleeding continued. Today, most surviving large kauri still bear notched scars.

A veteran gum-digger leans on his spade outside his corrugated iron shack in North Auckland.

burnt forest — layers of semi-fossilised resin shed from generations of kauri trees slowly became buried, first by accumulating forest litter, then by the passage of time. These deposits of kauri gum yielded to the probing spear and sharp spade of gum-diggers wherever kauri had once grown.

In reality, like gold-miners, few gum-diggers made their fortune, and life on the gum-fields was tough and physical. For many, scraping gum meant scraping by. It was the gum-buyers and exporters of Auckland City who did best out of kauri gum, valued for its use in varnishes, paints, and polishes. From 1850 to 1900, kauri gum dominated exports from Auckland Province, earning more than kauri timber, wool, or gold. Exports peaked in the early 1900s as uses found for kauri gum expanded (see opposite).

Digging up the past

Thirty-five years after Captain Cook misidentified kauri gum washed up on Northland beaches as an exudation from mangroves, Pakeha traders began investigating its

TYPES AND USES OF KAURI GUM

Types	Classes of gum (from highest to lowest quality) Grades (colour)		Uses	Main period of use (approx)
				1830–50, 1850–70, 1870–90, 1890–1910, 1910–30, 1930–50
RANGE & FOSSIL GUM	White (white to pale brown)	1921 30 grades	• marine glues	
	Amber (light or dark brown)		• high-grade oils/varnishes	
	Steel (burnt to glossy, clear to bottle green)		• paints & lacquers	
	Black (deep amber to dark brown)		• calico glazing	
			• dope for aircraft & fabric (First World War)	
BUSH GUM (fresh)	Virgin (bled)	1921 4 grades	• mouldings for dentures	
	Candle (trunk)			
	Crutch (forks of branches)			
SWAMP GUM	Chalky (roots & heart of tree)		• fire kindles	
	Sugar (black-jack)		• linoleum	
	Washed nuts/nubs		• low-grade varnishes	
	Chips & dust			
			MINOR USES & CURIOSITIES • weight-lifting talcum • heads of wax matches • cigar holders & pipestems • Pears & Sunlight soap • printing ink • souvenirs & jewellery • kauri 'hair'	

Although kauri gum never topped the national export charts, its overall monetary value to a struggling colonial economy (£45 million, over $83 million, between 1850 and 1930) was more than that contributed by the nineteenth-century gold rushes.

Sailing barque *Bjarne* loading gum being exported by Gillespie and Sons to New York from Auckland. The wharf is stacked with gum carefully packed (to prevent disintegration) in solid boxes made from heart kauri, which was often used to manufacture furniture when the gum reached its destination.

By the late nineteenth century, nearly everyone in Auckland Province was involved in the gum trade — skippers of coastal cutters and steamers took gum to Auckland city and returned to the gum-fields with supplies. The incoming gum was then sorted, cleaned, and graded by Auckland's ten major gum-buyers, ready for export.

commercial potential. The fledgling industry that developed in the 1830s to supply first American and later British varnish manufacturers relied on Bay of Islands Maori. Bartering kauri gum along with timber, flax, wheat, and potatoes for iron, muskets, and other European goods, local Maori made fortunes. By the mid-1840s, they were being paid cash at £5–£8 a tonne for cleaned gum. Even after the centre of the gum trade moved to Auckland in the 1840s, Maori continued to dominate the supply of gum, in the same way that they dominated the supply of kauri timber and agricultural produce to the merchants of the time.

Only after 1865, when gum prices almost doubled, did Pakeha consider 'the vagabond occupation' of gum-digging. Pakeha gum-diggers began working full-time on the gum-fields, first around Auckland and later in the Northern Wairoa and Mangawhai districts as the earlier fields became depleted. Increasing numbers of Maori also worked these gum-fields and continued to dominate in the Far North. Pakeha learnt the tricks of the trade from experienced Maori, who were particularly adept at identifying the root mounds that indicated the long-gone presence of a fallen kauri and at locating the direction in which the tree had fallen. Both root mound and where the tree crown had lain yielded large quantities of gum. At this time, Maori apparently cleaned their gum better than most Pakeha gum-diggers and generally received a small premium above the normal price.

In the 1870s, a system of leases and licences was put in place to check the unregulated fossicking by thousands of gum-diggers, who were destroying the topsoil with their digging and indiscriminately burning scrub — and sometimes forest. During the recurring economic hardships of

This 1919 advertisement takes advantage of the devastation caused by the 1918 flu epidemic to extol the virtues of an extract of kauri gum as a cough medicine — one of its more unusual uses.

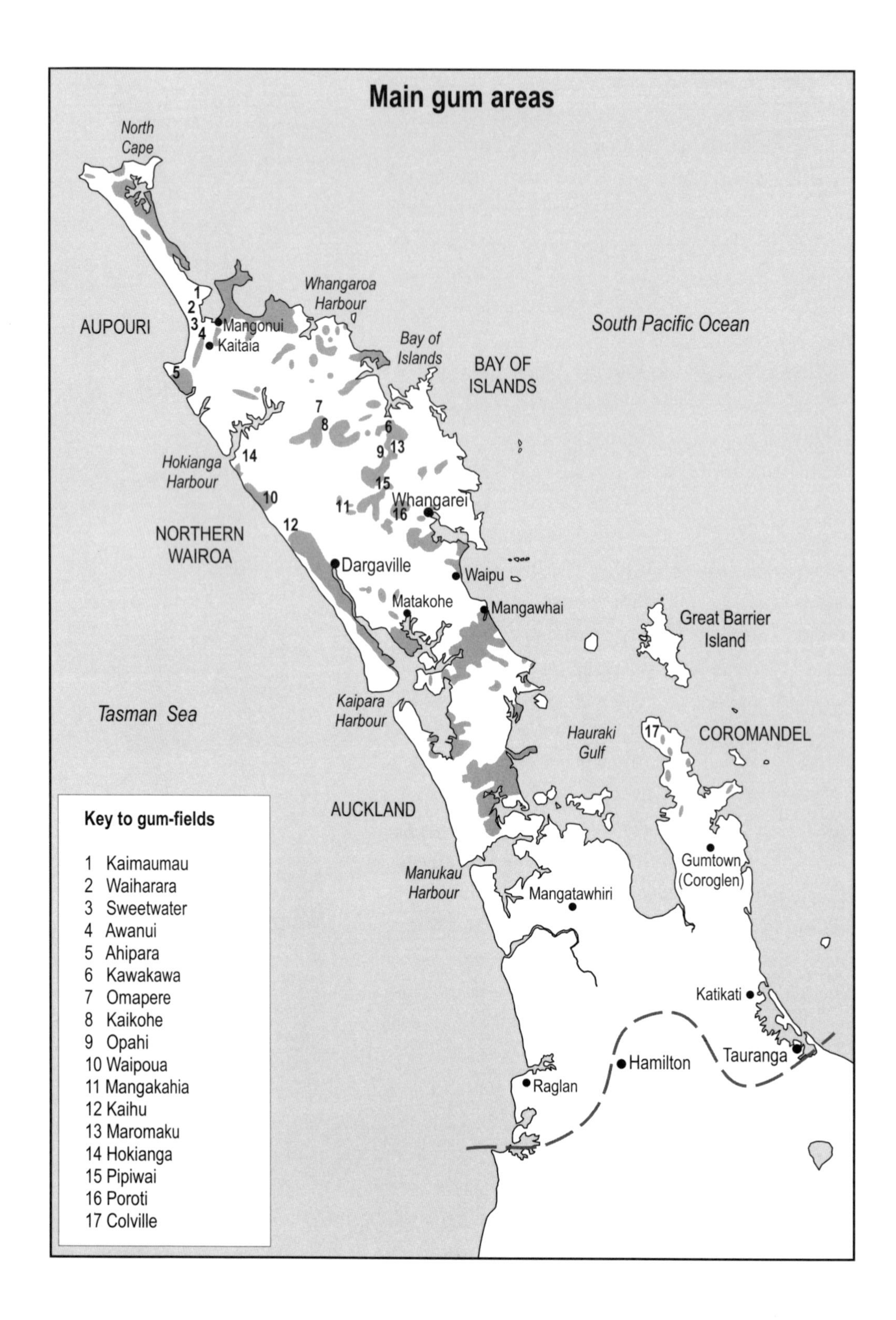
Main gum areas
North Cape
AUPOURI
Mangonui
Kaitaia
Whangaroa Harbour
Bay of Islands
BAY OF ISLANDS
South Pacific Ocean
Hokianga Harbour
NORTHERN WAIROA
Whangarei
Dargaville
Waipu
Matakohe
Mangawhai
Great Barrier Island
Tasman Sea
Kaipara Harbour
Hauraki Gulf
COROMANDEL
AUCKLAND
Manukau Harbour
Mangatawhiri
Gumtown (Coroglen)
Katikati
Tauranga
Hamilton
Raglan
1
2
3
4
5
6
7
8
9
10
11
12
13
14
15
16
17
Key to gum-fields
1 Kaimaumau
2 Waiharara
3 Sweetwater
4 Awanui
5 Ahipara
6 Kawakawa
7 Omapere
8 Kaikohe
9 Opahi
10 Waipoua
11 Mangakahia
12 Kaihu
13 Maromaku
14 Hokianga
15 Pipiwai
16 Poroti
17 Colville

the 1880s and 1890s, gum-fields throughout the kauri region (from the Far North to the Coromandel and Great Barrier Island, and south to Katikati and the Waikato) attracted up to 20,000 people — most of them part-time gum-diggers. Most Maori families north of Auckland were digging gum at this time. Their numbers were swelled by immigrants making a new start, gentlemen adventurers fallen on hard times, settlers supplementing marginal farm incomes, as well as unemployed and unemployable men from the city — the mix earning gum-diggers the reputation of being hard-drinking wastrels.

At the core of the industry from the 1890s to the 1930s were the 7000 full-time gum-diggers, many of whom were 'Austrian' migrants from the Dalmatian coast who had left a life of peasant farming to find their fortunes overseas. Their successful teamwork on the gum-fields caused resentment among Pakeha colonists. The Dalmatians were ostracised, penalised, and restricted in their endeavours well into the twentieth century, in much the same way — and for much the same reasons of fear, resentment, and envy — that the Chinese gold-miners of Otago were shunned and reviled.

But Dalmatians and Maori, the two groups of gum-diggers least well regarded by colonial New Zealand, formed the solid base of the gum industry and had the most lasting impact on the human landscape of the Far North.

Mixed Maori fortunes

In the 1830s, lumps of good-quality kauri gum lay on the surface. Gathering them could be fitted into the traditional seasonal round of work in the Bay of Islands — Maori gum-digging was mostly a summer occupation. Similarly, selling the gum followed traditional tribal practice. All the flax kete of gum gathered by one group were heaped up in front of the gum-buyer while their chief haggled for a good price — often paid in gold sovereigns. Each member of the group then filed past the buyer's clerk to receive what the chief considered their appropriate share.

Maori elsewhere soon took up gum-digging. As early as the mid-1840s, Ngati Whanaunga chief Te Horeta, who had provided the *Coromandel* with kauri spars in 1820 (see Chapter 4, The right stuff), set his people to gum-digging in the Colville area, Coromandel. Their activity renewed trouble over disputed land with Ngati Mahanga — not the only time that rights to increasingly valuable gum-fields were disputed (see this chapter, The last Maori war). Like other resources valued by Pakeha, kauri gum could become a pathway to prosperity and prestige.

After the focus of the trade shifted to Auckland, and competition among merchants increased the price in the 1850s, hundreds of Maori were attracted to the extensive gum-

Maori families set up temporary camps for the summer in the northern gum-fields, often living in tent-like shanties with sod chimneys. This gum-digging village is dated at about 1910.

At the end of a day's digging, the hard work of scraping dirt from the lumps of gum filled the evening. This veteran Maori gum-digger is posed with his scraping knife and a lump of gum held braced against a stick to gain maximum purchase.

fields around the city. By the mid-1860s, large areas of the northern wastelands were being dug over for gum. Maori travelled north to the gum-fields from as far south as Rotorua and Taupo — well outside their traditional tribal areas.

Changing fortunes

The increased demand for kauri gum after 1860 coincided with several emerging trends in Maori economics. By the late 1860s, Maori agriculture was losing its earlier dominance in the Auckland market. Maori wheat, often infested with weeds or diseased, fetched low export prices, and Maori seed potatoes had become riddled with eel-worm. Farming lost much of its appeal. With the onset of the New Zealand Wars, many Maori abandoned wheat production and disposed of their livestock. Maori dominance in coastal shipping was also weakening at this time as competition from now-established Pakeha traders and entrepreneurs became fiercer. By the end of the Wars, Maori traders were losing custom and Maori farmers affected by land confiscations were being forced to look for other sources of income.

Travelling long distances to work in the gum-fields continued for decades. Tribal connections lost some of their cohesiveness as groups of Maori from different areas banded together to dig gum, replacing the earlier pattern of chief-controlled groups. A vivid account of working in a group of unrelated Maori who came from all over the Waikato and Wanganui districts to the Kaipara gum-fields in the 1870s and 1880s was recorded in 1929. At the age of eight, Caroline Perrett was kidnapped in 1874 by Maori at Lepperton, Taranaki, in retaliation for her father clearing a Maori burial ground to prepare for a railway track. She lived the rest of her life as Maori. Later known as Mrs Ngoungou, she told of shifting from place to place in search of gum:

> *We lived in raupo whares and the life was hard and comfortless. Every morning, at daybreak, I used to go out with a spade and spear and dig until sunset. All the children worked just as hard as their parents. . . . In the evening we sat in the camp and scraped the gum. The dust and scrapings we flung on the fire which blazed up and lit the darkness. There were no candles at all.*
>
> *There was plenty of gum in those days . . . . When we had enough we took it down to the store and sold it . . . there was no township — only a shop or two. Our camp was ten miles from this place. . . . I used to walk the distance with about 60 lb of gum in a sack. . . . After selling the gum, we would each carry a 56 lb bag of flour back to the camp.*
>
> *As to clothes, I got just enough to keep me covered and no more. Print dresses, bought ready-made. . . . Boots I never saw at all. . . . My feet were as*

hard as iron and nothing could hurt them. About £1 was allowed me each time I sold my gum. The balance, in accordance with Maori custom, went towards the camp food.

(Mrs Ngoungou 1929)

At the same time that Waikato Maori started travelling north to dig gum, Hokianga Maori were also moving to the gum-fields, like those around Kaikohe and Lake Omapere, to help pay off debt as their income from trade in kauri timber dwindled (see Chapter 5, Energy and enterprise on the Hokianga). In the late 1850s, Te Rore Taoho (Te Roroa) put 200 gum-diggers from the Hokianga onto the Waipoua gum-fields. Another Te Roroa chief, Tiopira Kinaki, who had been involved with the Hokianga timber trade, was also digging gum around Waipoua at this time. By the depression years of the 1880s and 1890s, Maori from the Hokianga were working throughout the Waipoua, Mangakahia, and Northern Wairoa–Kaipara gum-fields. As John Klaricich explains:

It was only twenty years after the Land Wars [New Zealand Wars], and 1880 was a difficult year for Maori people from here [the Hokianga]. It was a drought year as well as a depression year — everything went wrong. All the adults went to where the gum-digging was on and left the children in the care of one family as a rule. If an accident occurred, a mother died or something, the children never got back to their own families. As a result our genealogy became a bit clouded during the gum-digging years.

Making good

By the 1890s, gum-fields could earn tribal land-holders considerable income — from being leased or sold, from royalties on the gum, and from the gum-digging efforts of their own people. The Poroti gum-field (inland from Whangarei), owned by Ngati Hine, was leased to gum-buyer Samuel Rawnsley, who collected licence fees of £1 per year from each digger, which went to the Maori owners (see this chapter, The last Maori war). The conditions of gum licences varied. At Poroti, a royalty of one shilling per hundredweight (ten cents per fifty kilograms) was deducted from the price paid for the gum, and the gum-diggers were obliged to sell to Rawnsley — acting as agent for the Maori owners. At this time about 100 gum-diggers, other than Maori, were paying licences and royalties on this gum-field.

Two prominent Ngati Hine families from Waiomio (inland Bay of Islands) — the Kopa (Cooper) and Kawiti Paraone (Brown) families moved to live near their gum-bearing land at Opahi at the start of the kauri boom. Jim Coffey (Ngati Hine) adds:

According to a kaumatua from Matawaia, Paki Korari, the locals came in on horseback to Opahi to dig and fossick for kapia or kauri gum . . . in the late 1800s and early 1900s. The kapia was loaded onto packhorses and taken into Kawakawa where it was weighed. This by-product . . . was extra income for the locals.

The descendants of these families continued to work in the kauri industry until the 1940s, and some of them still live in Opahi.

Proceeds from the Maromaku gum-field (near Motatau, inland from Kawakawa) were put to good use by the interconnected Ngati Hine families from the Matawaia–Pipiwai–Motatau area. These families all did well out of the gum-fields, many of them later building large houses and running substantial dairy herds on their farms. A typical story is that of the thrifty, hard-working, and indomitable matriarch, Pera Paraima (née Pera Hemi Tipene, widow of Te Piri Prime and Kevin Prime's grandmother). Pera earned enough from gum sales to pay off loans from the Department of Native Affairs that she had used to buy back and develop 4000 hectares of family land, sold under the Native Land Act 1909. Not trusting Pakeha banks, Pera used to store her wealth in Kapai biscuit tins in a locked storeroom. Tau Henare was one of her financial advisors, and Sir James Henare recounted a childhood memory of Pera consulting his father in 1916:

One day she arrived at our home with a 70-lb bag of gold sovereigns and half sovereigns, her earnings from gum-digging and the sale of fungus. She wanted my father to count them and when he next visited Kawakawa to deposit the lot in the bank to her credit. I remember this occasion vividly because my brother Brown and I enjoyed ourselves tossing coins all over the place.

Pera Paraima, indomitable and influential Ngati Hine matriarch (born 1876, died 1948), who bought back family land with money earned from her hard work in the gum-fields.

Despite spending most of her married life in a dirt-floored hut in a forest clearing — where most of her fifteen children were born — by about 1920, the now-widowed Pera Paraima had accumulated enough wealth to build a substantial villa of kauri, and was milking 100 cows as well as running beef cattle and sheep. She continued farming her recouped land until her death in 1948 at the age of seventy-two (see also Chapter 8, The last of the obsolete cowboys and Chapter 9, Community, commemoration, and culture).

From vineyard to gum-field

Lured by the opportunity of making a new life overseas, many impoverished people from the Dalmatian coast of Croatia travelled to the gum-fields of Northland. By the 1890s, increasing numbers of young single men were leaving their homes in Austrian-annexed Catholic Dalmatia in response to over-population, marginal farming on fragmented small-holdings, disease-devastated grapevines, the threat of military service, and the prospect of El Dorado in foreign parts. Mostly peasant farmers, they left a subsistence life to earn a quick buck wherever they could find employment — in the Americas, Australia, and New Zealand. As Drago Yelavich of Kaitaia explains:

> *Families and villages tended to go to the same place as that was the one they heard about. My Dad, Stipan Yelavich, was born in inland Dalmatia at Ravca in 1894. He first went to Western Australia in 1912 [aged eighteen], then came here in 1915.*

Many of those who came to the northern gum-fields did not intend settling. They sent most of their earnings home to support their families, returning to Dalmatia after three or four years when they had made a modest 'fortune'. Some stayed only because they did not earn enough to pay the return passage. Others were joined by family members. Stipan Yelavich first joined brother Ante, then went north to the gum-fields with cousins Peter and Tony Yelavich. The fathers of Milan Jurlina (of Sweetwater) and John Klaricich (of Hokianga) — both from Zivogosce — were sent to New Zealand in the early 1900s aged thirteen, either with family members or to join those already here. Of the four other Klaricich brothers who left home at the same time, one came to New Zealand, two went to Terra del Fuego (Chile), and the fourth returned to Dalmatia.

By the early 1900s, several thousand Dalmatians were working on the northern gum-fields, moving when and where new gum-fields were discovered. Their lack of English, foreign lifestyle, segregation in camps with their fellow countrymen, and their habit of finding quantities of gum on patches apparently already worked out, did not endear them to xenophobic British gum-diggers. Perhaps worst of all, nine of them had the gall to win £9000 in a Tattersall's racing sweep in 1892, some of which was promptly sent home to

Only British settlers, naturalised foreigners, and Maori were allowed annual gum licences at a cost of five shillings (fifty cents) to work on Crown reserves or in State Forests like Puhipuhi. Dalmatians and other aliens could dig only on non-reserved Crown land or on Maori and private land — and then only after they had been in the country for three months and had paid a much higher annual licence fee of £1 ($2).

THE KAURI GUM INDUSTRY AMENDMENT ACT. 1902.

178

License for State Forests.

J A Skinner of Puhi Puhi having this day paid the sum of TWENTY SHILLINGS, is hereby authorised and licensed to dig for Kauri Gum within the Puhi Puhi State Forest, subject to the provisions of "The Kauri Gum Industry Act, 1898," and its Amendments and Regulations for the time being in force thereunder. This License continues in force from the 1st day of May, 1903 until the 30th day of September, 1903.

Dated this 28th day of May 1903.

Commissioner of Crown Lands.

Printed at the Observer Office, Auckland.

Dalmatia. Antipathy grew throughout the 1890s. The Dalmatian gum-diggers were subjected to loudly voiced resentment from the newly set up Gum-diggers Union and from major gum-buyers such as Joseph Evans at Royal Commissions convened for the purpose. Although Dalmatian industriousness, honesty, and frugality were grudgingly acknowledged, it was thought that the colony gained nothing from their efforts. They paid no taxes, built no roads, developed no farmland. A blasted heath riddled with deep holes was the only sign of their fleeting presence.

The result was the creation of Kauri Gum Reserves on the best gum-bearing Crown land — over 100,000 hectares — from which aliens were excluded under the Kauri Gum Industry Act 1898. Despite ongoing legal discrimination of this sort, Dalmatian gum-diggers continued their efforts, with many of those who came after 1900 becoming naturalised citizens. Clem Jurlina became a British citizen in 1907, four years after his arrival, his naturalisation certificate still the proud possession of son Milan.

In the Far North after the turn of the century, Dalmatian migrants congregated in small townships like Waiharara, Waipapakauri, Waihopo, and Ahipara, where their continued isolation from British gum-diggers created strong bonds with local Maori. Many Dalmatian men married into local families. The two peoples learnt each other's language (Maori still call Dalmatians 'Tarara[ra]' in imitation of their rapid-fire speech) and Maori often worked for Dalmatians on the gum-fields. Today, many northern Maori families have Dalmatian surnames and many Dalmatian families have Maori cousins — lasting reminders of the mingling of two ethnic groups from very different origins as the result of shared adversity and family-oriented communal lifestyles.

Life in the windswept north

The northernmost gum-fields — those on the Aupouri Peninsula and around Kaitaia — were the last worked. They reached their peak in the 1920s–1930s, when there were about thirty gum-stores, many shops and post offices, and seven dance halls in the district. Here, the Dalmatians came into their own, using mechanised sluicing operations to retrieve large quantities of the now-valuable gum chips used in the linoleum industry.

In the 1920s, about nine Dalmatian and Maori 'gangs' worked the shallow gum-field on Ahipara Hill. At first, both single men and families lived in the typical gum-field shacks made from new jute sacks stretched on a tea-tree frame. Cheap at sixpence to one shilling (five to ten cents) each, about twenty sacks made an adequate shack — the steep-pitched sacking roof became surprisingly waterproof once rain had shrunk it taut. Once a little money was coming in, improvements were made — first a corrugated iron roof and chimney, then walls, interior match-lining, and wooden floors.

Life for married women was hard. On Ahipara Hill, water had to be carried from a well, the rudimentary sanitary facilities were outside, and hot water was boiled in a kerosene tin or a copper. Nellie Jelecich (née Yelavich) recalls that they were unable to afford transport to the doctor at Kaitaia, and used traditional herbal remedies recorded in Dalmatian medical books, growing herbs like chamomile for stomach and period pains. Maori medical lore was also shared with the Dalmatians. Plants like kumarahou (the leaves still used by Maori for relief from respiratory complaints and for general health) became known as gum-digger's soap as the crushed leaves and flowers made a cleansing lather. Children were born on the gum-field, often with the help of a Maori midwife, and children died on the gum-field. Three of Drago Yelavich's siblings were born on Ahipara Hill; two of his sisters died there.

Good at handwork, the Dalmatian women sewed and knitted, gathering snagged wool from the tea-tree and spinning it onto hand-held bobbins (kudja). As much as possible, they replicated home in the barren scrubland. Travellers in Northland today can recognise places where Dalmatians once lived by the surviving fig trees and grapevines. Drago Yelavich recalls:

> *Virtually every household had a house cow. The cows never roamed far because they were fed from their gardens and they would come to their call. They all had big gardens, planted fruit trees and a grapevine. You wouldn't be Dalmatian without a grapevine and a fig tree. They grew their own type of cabbage, picked leaf by leaf — rustica, or Dallie cabbage. That's still grown, the seed gets handed on. Garlic and a beautiful runner bean. They made their own bread, their own wine — made gallons of it every year, brewed their own beer, distilled their own spirits (illegal, of course!).*

Even bachelor Dalmatian men often lived well by the standards of the gum-fields, making their own bread in camp ovens and putting up supplies of wine, beer, and spirits. This baker (possibly Urlich) stands outside his neatly organised shanty and campsite on Ahipara Hill about 1910.

Drago's wife, Anna, points out that Dalmatians on remote gum-fields drank wine and coffee made with milk, cooked with olive oil, and ate sun-dried tomatoes two generations before these became sophisticated café fare in New Zealand. Clem Jurlina used to stock gallon tins of olive oil in his store at Sweetwater, and Milan has kept the rusted tin coffee-bean roaster mounted on a spit handle that his mother used over her open cooking fire.

Growing up on the gum-fields

In general, Dalmatian women did not work on the gum-fields, although they sometimes collected gum 'nuts' from the ground after the sluicing, and the 'chalk' gum that floated to the top during washing was seen as their perk for Christmas. In contrast, Maori women spent as much time down gum-holes as their men. Eighty-six-year-old Mrs Kate Phillips (née Milich) of Ahipara remembers her Maori mother and Dalmatian father digging gum on the Kaimaumau gum-fields when they lived at Waiharara in the 1920s. She picked gum nuts herself as a child:

> *I was eight or nine when I started. We used to nut pick every summer school holidays, for six or seven weeks. The four of us children could fill a big sack*

This well-known Northwood photograph of Liza Tahi posed in a gum swamp about 1910 with her spade, spear, and flax kete has lost none of its charm.

> *every week. . . . The Dalmatians had the big machines and that, and we used to pick up the nuts from the earth the machines would turn up. When it rained, the gum nuts would wash out of that earth and show up. We worked from breakfast until after dark.*

Later, she moved with her mother and younger sister (Mrs Florrie Berghan of Ahipara) to the Northern Wairoa where Neta Milich had some land. There they continued gum-digging:

> *I've got some scars on my foot where I dug the spade into it. I liked digging gum. I knew how to find gum with a spear. There were areas where we could go to dig gum. But that's all gone now, all into farms.*

Both sisters learned to weave flax from their mother, who made money weaving floor mats for gum-diggers' shacks and kete for gum and shopping. Both still weave and do other handwork today. But a child's life on the gum-fields was not all hard work. The sisters remember scrambling on the parasitic konene creeper that still covers the tea-tree scrub and eating its yellowy-green berries, sucking the juice out of flax stalks and flowers. As Florrie Berghan recalls:

We did lots of things, made our own fun. Everyone had a horse or two — in our day it was all tea-tree, wiwi, and fern, and our horses ran wild. We little kids could catch those horses — once you threw a rope across their backs, they wouldn't run away. Sometimes we would ride out to Ninety Mile Beach to get toheroas. We would just use a bridle made of flax tied together, no saddle. On our way to school there was a place where the Dallies had dug out a huge kauri log. When the place where the log had been filled with water, we used to swim there. We taught ourselves.

Digging for gum became part of the northern Maori lifestyle. This family is sorting and scraping gum at Parengarenga, the most northern settlement on the Aupouri Peninsula.

Born to wheel and deal

As part of his business buying gum from the Kaimaumau, Ahipara, and other local gum-fields, Clem Jurlina became a fluent Maori speaker. After trying his luck on the gum-fields with an older brother for a few years, he had soon become a trader — because, according to Roy Wagener, 'he couldn't keep himself in sugar, digging gum'. He began with two or three tins of biscuits and bully beef under his bunk in his shack, then branched out from that. By the 1930s, when the major gum-buyers all worked out of Auckland, Clem Jurlina and Sons based at Sweetwater was probably the biggest storekeeper and buyer left in the north. As Milan Jurlina explains:

> *When the old uncle died, my father took over the business here [at Sweetwater]. He exported all over the world — United States, India, Sweden, Italy. . . . My father also sold everything a gum-digger needed. He was always a born wheeler and dealer. My mother used to complain that even if she asked Dad to keep something new from the shop for her, he'd sell the last one in stock if a buyer came in — he couldn't resist.*

The gum-buying season was at its busiest just before Christmas, when the gum-digging gangs had finished drying and winnowing their stockpiled gum chips. After digging the hill and range terrain through the wet winter months and working the swamps in drier weather, the gangs spent the spring machine-washing the gum out of their piled-up 'walls' of cut sods. The washed gum was then spread to dry in 'tips' on level high ground. As Milan Jurlina explains:

> *We'd be on the road [buying at the tips] almost every day, if we weren't here [at the Sweetwater depot] sorting and bagging. . . . We always hand-filled our bags and packed them down hard. We'd ram the bags solid, get in four or five kilos extra.*

The Jurlinas had their gum-works at the foot of the Sweetwater Hill, where they boiled the gum in salt water in big kauri vats, skimming the buoyant cleaned gum off the surface. The bagged gum was sent by railway line to Awanui, where it was stored to be collected by scows and coastal steamers (mostly owned by the well-known Subritzky family, still in shipping today), then taken to Auckland.

Milan still lives on the family land at Sweetwater. Near his modern brick home stands the small weatherboard cottage — with its espaliered grapevines on either side of the path and its sheltering fig tree — where Clem and Karmela Jurlina brought up their family of five. Nearby is his father's office. The walls are festooned with dockets and correspondence from all over the world, bulldog-clipped onto nails, the old desk and shelves piled high with memorabilia. Across the road, the original store shed is still full of gum-digging equipment and bagged kauri gum — the largest remaining stockpile in the country. With the introduction of cheap synthetics soon after the Second World War, the market for kauri gum slowly dwindled and died, until only the most specialised uses still attracted buyers. Milan Jurlina comments:

> *I was still selling the odd bag of high-grade gum in the mid-1990s. That was going to Europe for restoring furniture and for violin makers. They still claim that the kauri gum varnishes produce the best sound.*

As a new component in the traditional competition between chiefs, the ownership of muskets contributed to the temporary escalation of conflict in the 1820s that became known as the Musket Wars. **(Chapter 4, Maori dynamics and the Musket Wars)**

Sketched by Charles Heaphy in 1839, this view is of the timber yard at Kohukohu on the Hokianga (then owned by G. F. Russell, whose house is shown). The *Francis Speight* is taking kauri logs on board through her stern loading port — the limitations of these ports later caused John Webster much anxiety. **(Chapter 5, Energy and enterprise on the Hokianga)**

Charles Heaphy's 1839 picture of pit-sawyers in dense kauri forest on the Wairoa River, in the Kaipara, reveals the labour-intensive nature of their work. **(Chapter 5, Getting into gear)**

John Webster, owner of the sawmill at Kohukohu on the Hokianga, painted at the time of his wedding in 1855 or a few years later. **(Chapter 5, Energy and enterprise on the Hokianga)**

Augustus Earle's painting of the shipyard at Horeke (then known as Deptford) in the Hokianga, 1827, with the *New Zealander*, the second kauri ship to be built there, on the stocks.

(Chapter 5, Sailing ships and shipbuilders)

Kawiti's strategic pa at Ruapekapeka was designed with deep bunkers to withstand the British bombardment of January 1846. After two weeks, Kawiti and Hone Heke partially abandoned the pa in a feigned retreat. The battle ended in an inconclusive victory for the British. Peace brokered shortly afterwards by Nene ended the Northern War.

(Chapter 6, Prestige, power and politics)

Now collectors' pieces, elegant Victorian furniture was made from kauri and other native timbers by craftsmen like William Norrie.

(Chapter 6, Capitalising on kauri)

Kiln-drying and modern machinery now allow specialist furniture-makers to transform 35–45,000-year-old swamp kauri into superb furniture. One such company, Davies Furniture of Christchurch, makes classic kauri furniture based on traditional designs and techniques used by the Davies' ancestor Robert Norrie in the 1890s (a brother of William Norrie — see Chapter 6, Capitalising on kauri). Pieces of Norrie furniture still grace the Davies family homes and the Norrie tradition of fine furniture-making has passed down each generation to the present.

By the mid 1980s, regenerating kauri forests, like this one in the rugged landscape of the Coromandel, had been brought under the protection of forest park status. **(Chapter 9, Shifting shoals)**

A garden escapee, wild ginger has invaded many pristine native habitats, including kauri forest at Waipoua, Waima, and Mataraua. **(Chapter 10, Sinister forces)**

Damage caused by possums is one of the major threats facing New Zealand's forest ecosystems. High possum numbers reduce the food supply for native birds such as kokako and kukupa as well as contributing to forest degradation, such as this 1994 scene of possum-killed trees in the Manaia Forest Sanctuary, Coromandel. **(Chapter 10, Sinister forces)**

An ancient Gondwana relict species associated with kauri forest, the giant carnivorous kauri snail (pupurangi) that feeds on insects and worms is itself vulnerable to predation by wild pigs.

(Chapter 10, Sinister forces)

A Kauri 2000 Trust volunteer plants kauri seedlings on a line cut through scrub on a Coromandel site.

(Chapter 10, Kauri forests for the future)

Te Ao o Nga Atua – Cliff Whiting's modern mural depicting the world of the gods is carved in kauri timber.

Clem Jurlina (far right) buying bagged gum from some Maori gum-diggers at a gum-drying tip in Northland. Steelyards with scales, and later more sophisticated weighing machines, were used to weigh representative bags of gum at the drying tips. Negotiated prices were then based on the number of filled bags. The Jurlina family were well known for ramming the bags solid to gain extra weight for their money.

Moving on

From the gum-fields, most Dalmatians moved on to other occupations, many buying small parcels of worked-over gum-land and developing farms, orchards, and vineyards. Most northern dairy farmers started as gum-diggers, using proceeds from gum to pay off the land. Gum-buyer Clem Jurlina bought land at Awanui, his sons taking up milking in the 1950s when the gum business dwindled, eventually farming 200 hectares — where Milan and his son now run 500 beef cattle. Others moved to fishing and trucking; some ran boarding houses and restaurants. After fifteen years on Ahipara Hill, Stipan and Perina Yelavich moved to Awanui, where they ran a boarding house, fish-shop/restaurant, and attached billiard saloon and hairdressers until their retirement in 1969.

Drago and Milan's generation of Dalmatians have kept their heritage alive in a modern world. Many still speak the language and participate in annual festivals that feature embroidered costumes, tamburica orchestras, and kolo dancing, sustained by traditional feasting on spit-roast lamb, camp-oven potatoes, Dallie cabbage, and runner beans. They are proud of their achievements in all walks of life. Today's New Zealand Dalmatian community has come a long way from its impoverished beginnings on the gum-fields.

THE LAST MAORI WAR

The gum-fields between Poroti and Pipiwai were considered of such value that two Ngati Hine hapu took up muskets in 1898 to determine who had prior rights to proceeds from the gum. Erima Henare (Ngati Hine) explains:

> *After gathering at their respective marae, war parties from Te Uriroroi of Poroti and Te Orewai of Pipiwai fought a pitched battle at Purua, in Mangakahia. Four men were killed, three from Te Uriroroi, before peace was finally settled by an envoy from Maihi Paraone Kawiti, the chief of Ngati Hine at the time. The marae at Poroti is still named Te Maungarongo, 'the enduring peace', for the peace-making. The muskets used by both sides in the battle lie buried nearby, the tapu location kept secret.*

As a skirmish over land rights and resources, this was a traditional Maori battle. Known throughout the north as the last Maori war, it was probably the last such battle fought in New Zealand.

The Orewai war party armed with muskets and staves outside the Pipiwai marae before the battle at Purua. Uto Peeni (extreme right) — Erima Henare's great-great uncle — was the one fatality from this group. Wero, Panapa, and Hemi Tau Rapunga of Te Uriroroi were also killed.

CHAPTER 8

The cutting edge

PEAK AND DECLINE OF THE
KAURI TIMBER INDUSTRY, 1900–1940

Driving forces

Massive timbers thrust upwards, their skeletal outline stark against the sky. Rusted wire hawsers or cables suspend a fringe of rough-hewn planks from the lowest and biggest of five cross beams or stringers. The ends of the planks butt onto a huge kauri log that spans the narrow gorge, a metre above the surface of the creek. Beyond the black shadows underneath, the clear water barely ripples as it slides around pot-holed bed-rock and over drifts of golden pebbles. The serenity of this bush-framed scene seems incongruous against the brooding remains of the man-made structure.

Hidden in dense bush up the Kaiarara Valley on Great Barrier Island, this decaying structure is all that remains of one of the largest kauri driving dams ever built. Constructed for contractor George Murray by Eb Gibbons and son Jack Murray about 1926, it was one of seven dams used to flush kauri logs down the creeks in the steep and rugged terrain of the Kaiarara catchment in the 1920s. Only the main structural timbers of the forty-metre wide and fourteen-metre high dam have survived, now partially restored and preserved by the Historic Places Trust and the Department of Conservation.

The partially restored fourteen-metre high, forty-metre wide main dam in the Kaiarara Valley, Great Barrier Island.

High on the ridges of the Coromandel, another large kauri dam was partially restored and preserved in 1994. The Dancing Camp dam can be reached after a two- to three-hour tramp in the Kauaeranga Valley, just east of Thames. Built by Jim Angel in 1924, it was the second-largest dam in the Kauaeranga watershed.

These two timber dams are among the few still-substantial remains of the estimated 3000 driving dams built during the kauri era and were among the last to be constructed. Dams were most extensively used in the steep terrain of the Coromandel, the Waitakere Ranges (Auckland), and around the Hokianga, and less extensively throughout the rest of the kauri region. Most of these timber structures have now succumbed to floodwaters, weather, and time. Often all that remains is the sill log or the notches cut in bedrock to take the timber beams. In the Kauaeranga, most of the more than fifty dams built at various times have disappeared or are in poor condition.

Only at Dancing Camp or Kaiarara can the visitor easily imagine something of the awe-inspiring force of water released from such dams to carry kauri logs down the steep creeks to the sea. But some of the bushmen recorded photographic sequences and descriptions that bring the kauri drives to life.

Letting go

Although many dams were tripped singly, sequential or simultaneous dam releases on adjacent creeks involved careful planning and coordination. The build-up to a big drive took months, sometimes years. Only when as many logs as possible lay piled in the dry creek beds below the dams, filled the pools above the dams, and waited along the creek banks to be levered into the water, did the drive begin. H. E. Hewlett describes a drive on the Wharekawa River, Coromandel:

> *. . . On the right, the last of the timber from Brown's dam was thundering past. . . . As the clamour of the right died down, another uproar arose — on the left — the sound of innumerable logs thundering against each other, driven by the violence of the water. Then a wall of water and logs, many feet in height, came into sight, and beneath the westering moon, we saw thousands of logs go past. They seemed to be alive, grumbling and complaining in their discomfort and agony. Great logs were driven high up on the bank, swung round, and torn away again. Long logs, their butts driven into the bed of the creek, rose up on end, and fell over again, until the whole mighty mass had gone thundering down the main Wharekawa to the salt water.*
>
> (Reed 1964)

Above Using timber jacks, these men are moving a large kauri log into a driving creek in the Kauaeranga Valley, Coromandel, in 1922.

Opposite Water bursts from the gate as the Dancing Camp dam is tripped in the head of the Kauaeranga Valley, in 1924.

Wet and winter cold often added to the dangerous work of tripping the gate and prodding logs towards the flume or chute from the narrow top of a dam structure already shuddering from the force of the released water and the weight of logs. Even after a successful drive, the bushmen had to retrieve logs flung high onto the banks by the maelstrom of water that treated ten-tonne logs like matchsticks. They often had to tackle logs jammed against an unforeseen obstruction — sometimes in the gate of the dam itself. Using timber jacks (and sometimes dynamite) to separate tangled logs and lever them back into the creek bed was known as 'trimming', and was often precarious work. It could take months before all the salvaged logs were tipped back into the creeks ready for the next drive.

Many logs were never retrieved; others so battered they were not worth retrieving. They still lie today, stranded in the bush high above the creek beds — mute testimony to the force of a drive. Despite the effectiveness of drives in moving thousands of logs at a time, they could be expensive in wasted timber and wasted effort. As many as thirty to forty percent

Untangling log jams after a drive was often precarious and dangerous work. This ingenious contraption of ropes and levers was known as a 'bush devil'.

of the logs were lost or destroyed, higher percentages still in drives down steep and narrow gorges and over waterfalls. Ninety percent of the logs felled in the Billy Goat Basin (upper Kauaeranga) some time in the 1880s did not survive the first attempt to drive them over the Billy Goat Falls — a loss of more than 200 cubic metres of kauri timber. As a result, efforts in the Basin were abandoned for forty years, despite the alluring stands of kauri present.

By the late nineteenth century, inaccessible or treacherous terrain like that of the Billy Goat was often all that stood between the twenty-five percent of kauri forest left and the determined loggers. But the Melbourne-based Kauri Timber Company's purchase of sawmills and cutting rights over 180,000 hectares of kauri forest in 1889 drove men and machines in a renewed effort to extract the last of the kauri. A final accelerated wave of cutting, extraction, and milling of kauri of all sizes (down to diameters of thirty centimetres) swept inexorably through terrain that had been logged before and terrain that had earlier been considered unloggable.

Last frontiers

As part of this final wave, the steepest reaches of the Kauaeranga in the Coromandel and the Kaiarara on Great Barrier Island were logged in the twenty years after the First World War. In these years alone, 217,000 cubic metres of kauri timber (enough to build 9000 modern houses) were taken out of the Kauaeranga. From the Kaiarara and adjacent watersheds, the last of Great Barrier Island's economically millable kauri (130,000 cubic metres or 5500 houses) was retrieved. At the end of 130 years of logging on Great Barrier, the only significant stand of kauri left untouched was on the summit of Mt Hobson itself — its almost vertical volcanic dome and stumpy ancient trees (some dated as 700 years old) putting it beyond the attention of even the most intrepid tree feller.

A big drive in the Kauaeranga in 1921 yielded 13,000 cubic metres of logs, seen here backed up behind the booms.

Practice and pragmatism

As the terrain became more difficult, driving dams and bush tramways reached high levels of design and skill; levels that owed nothing to engineering blueprints or sophisticated calculations but everything to experience. The builders of dams and tramways were usually experienced bushmen rather than specialists, though those who earned the reputation for excellence were in demand — the success of a logging operation hinged on the reliability of its extraction structures. George Murray, in charge of the Great Barrier operation and its Kaiarara dams, was a master axeman long before he became a dam-builder and contractor. A keen eye and superior skills with timber and tools were certainly major prerequisites.

The building of a dam was a massive undertaking, taking several months and using large amounts of kauri timber. The Dancing Camp dam used seventy cubic metres of kauri — enough timber to build three substantial houses, all of it felled and pit-sawn on the spot — and this dam was not as large as the main dam in the Kauaeranga or the Kaiarara. Most dams were used over and over again until all the timber had been cut from the catchment and driven down the creeks.

In terrain too steep or rugged for bullock teams, getting the logs to the creeks and main

A swinging rafter dam being built in the Kauaeranga in 1920. The men on the beam are using timber jacks to lever one of the swinging rafters into position over the gateway. The planked walls need to be caulked and any leaks sealed by dumping 'bukau' (fibrous litter from the mound at the base of kauri trees) into the dam pool — the matted material becoming pressed like a poultice against the dam wall by water pressure.

The just-completed main dam in the Kauaeranga, with some logs already lined up in the slowly filling dam pool. Such dams sloped about sixty degrees downstream, needing to be back-braced by solid struts.

waterways often required ingenious engineering solutions. Timber-lined chutes and wide rolling roads — down which men skilled with timber-jacks would sequentially move up to 100 logs at a time — had been used extensively in the Coromandel. But by the 1920s, steam-haulers and tramways were being combined as the most effective means of delivering logs to the waterways. Some of these tramways required the construction of viaducts or trestle bridges over gullies, and they all required accurate cambering and calculation of slope ratios. Like the dams, tramways were purpose-built from available material. Their builders surveyed and cleared the route, then used kauri trees growing on site for all the structural components. At one stage, even the lengths of tramline and sleepers were pit-sawn as well as all the bridge timbers. Later, iron rails were used.

In an industry fraught with danger, being a brakeman on these tramways was one of the most dangerous jobs of all. Often relying on gravity, the speed of the logs had to be controlled by these brakemen, who rode on the bogies (wheeled undercarriages) to operate the brake levers. Even when the terrain was too steep for gravity operation, and the bogies were controlled by steam-hauler, brakemen still sometimes rode with the logs.

Cutting on contract

Top bushmen often took on Kauri Timber Company (KTC) logging contracts for large tracts of government-owned land. They used their experience to calculate the most effective ways and means of extracting the contracted amount of timber from the hillside and delivering it to the booms — for the price of about ten shillings (about a dollar) per cubic metre. If that were not enough of a challenge, the contractor had to hire the men involved in all aspects of the work, provide them with the necessary equipment, then house and feed them sufficiently well to keep them on the job for months at a time. Although the men's wages and expenses were covered by Company cheques, the contractor reaped his own reward only on final delivery at the end of the contract. It was not a venture for the financially faint-hearted.

One of the best-known contractors, Bert Collins (older brother of photographer/bushman Tudor Collins), seemed to thrive on such challenges. In 1920, he won the largest KTC contract ever offered — logging 184,000 cubic metres from the Kauaeranga. Nearly half the timber was in the steep rugged mountain country above the Gorge, including the coveted stands in the Billy Goat Basin, above the notorious timber-smashing waterfall. By using a combination of steam-haulers and tramways, Collins succeeded in extracting most of the trees from the basin — an estimated 9000–12,000 cubic metres. By 1928, the contract was completed, most of the kauri had been logged, and the bushmen left the Kauaeranga.

In the late 1930s, Bert Collins was the contractor for one of the last known areas in which driving dams were used. By this time, steam-haulers and bulldozers had taken over most of the extraction tasks in the bush. But an area being logged near Katikati, the most southern kauri forest, had been abandoned at the start of the First World War. The contractor had lost most of his men to the armed forces — leaving the creeks filled with logs. Building four dams, Collins drove out the logs felled twenty-five years earlier — as well as 55,000 cubic metres of newly felled kauri:

> *His largest drive there was an involuntary one, when a flash flood overfilled all the dams and he had to release them all together . . . more than 1500 cubic metres of logs, shooting down in the floodwaters, smashed the booms . . . and ended up scattered around Tauranga harbour.*
>
> (Halkett and Sale 1986)

From the Katikati contract, Collins moved on to Northland (to the Mangakahia area and finally to Kaihu, near Waipoua Forest). In these areas, much of the logging in the 1920s and 1930s was on land that had been sold under the Native Lands Act 1909 — with most of the logs going to the Kauri Timber Company. Much of the remaining forested land in Maori

LOGGING THE KAUAERANGA

In the 1920s, logs were hauled from the head of the Kauaeranga Basin to the top of the Billy Goat tramway, where they were loaded on the bogies seen at the right of the picture. The hauler is in the shed with the smoke stack. In the background, Jim O'Neill's bush camp shanties line the edge of the clearing.

The spectacular Billy Goat tramway and incline were constructed to bypass the obstacle of the Billy Goat Falls in 1921. Restored remnants of this tramway — kauri trestle bridges (one 160 metres long and 11 metres above the ground), deep cuttings blasted through solid rock, and stretches of surviving kauri sleepers — can be seen from walking tracks that start from the Kauaeranga road end. Kauri logs on bogies are on the way down the incline, with others piled at the bottom of the incline waiting to be hauled the short distance to the main river.

These logs are being hauled through a short canal dug to connect the main Kauaeranga Valley booms with the loading skids beside the Kauaeranga tramway. This canal was part of a complex extraction network that used log chutes, skidded roads, dams, and tramways.

A bush locomotive on the main Kauaeranga tramway in 1922, with driver Bill Nankivell seated on the right on the log. Built between 1914 and 1921, this twenty-three kilometre-long tramway transported its loads of logs to booms on the Waihou River, near Thames.

ownership was also being logged, with local Maori providing most of the workforce.

Logging in the Pipiwai–Motatau forests (east of Mangakahia) that Ngati Hine owned had started during the First World War, reaching its peak in the 1920s and 1930s. Logs from the western side of the Motatau catchment were hauled to the Kaikou River for driving down to the Northern Wairoa mills (see Chapter 5, Working the Kaipara waterways). Logs from the eastern side were hauled to rail sidings at Motatau and Opahi or to roads where trucks could take them to the nearest mill — owned by Tau Henare, who had the KTC contract for the area.

Better known as a politician, Tau Henare had first worked as a kauri bushman. When Sir Peter Buck retired from public life, northern Maori consulted a tohunga or seer for advice on his successor. Tau Henare's grandson Erima explains:

> *The seer, Matekino Hauraki, had a vision of a tall fair man working deep in the bush. With the people, she scoured the bush to find him. She recognised Tau Henare as the man in her vision. He was working in the Northern Wairoa at the time.*

After Tau went into politics, the mill was run by his son Henare Henare (Sir James's brother) with Elwyn Carter — founder of Carter Holt Harvey, which now has major pine forests in the area.

The last of the obsolete cowboys

In these Ngati Hine forests, the logs were hauled by bullock teams up to the late 1940s, when they were competing against tractor-haulers. Jim Coffey (Ngati Hine) explains:

> *My father, Kawhi (Bill Coffey), was known as the last of the obsolete cowboys. His team of bullocks hauled logs where bulldozers feared to tread — through narrow gullies and inaccessible goat tracks, skirting around swamps and wading through creeks — much to the dismay of the modern haulage contractors, who would take an extra day to find dry ground for their machines to traverse.*

Kawhi (Bill Coffey) aged about twenty-one with one of his beloved bullocks in the early 1940s.

As a teenager, Kawhi had learned his trade working as an offsider for his grandfather,

Rongo Kawiti Brown, who had had a team of bullocks in the early 1900s. By the time Kawhi was seventeen, he was a droving contractor with his own team.

Prime Cooper's uncle, bushman Sam Prime (Kevin Prime's father), also had a bullock team in the area, and he remembers seeing kauri logs on catamarans or sledges being skidded out of bush on family land. Sam Prime's sisters had the job of pouring buckets of water on the skids to make the log slide easier. Prime Cooper recalls:

> *They made the skids hinuhinu [greasy]. The most important bullocks were the lead pair and the pair that brought up the rear — they had to hold their ground whenever the team changed direction, before the log could be pulled in the new direction.*

Kawhi's bullocks were hand-reared and would respond to their names and pair off when called. The first two leaders, the strongest and the most intelligent, paired off first, followed by the others in order of their strength and abilities. All the yokes were hand-carved and tailor-made for each beast. Kawhi never used force or a whip to drive his team. As Jim Coffey says:

> *They thrived on the master's touch and his T.L.C. When the team was in full flight and he wanted them to turn left or right, he would call out to the leading pair, 'E Hori, huri mai' or 'E Niko, huri atu', and the leaders would force the whole team to turn left or right without missing a beat.*

Kawhi's assistant, his 'offsider', had the responsibility of working out the safest way through the bush a day before the journey — no skidded roads for this bullock team. The offsider also had to find campsites and grazing for the animals along the way. Kawhi and his offsider took a packhorse with them, loaded with bedding, cooking utensils, and basic food supplies. In contrast to the fare expected in the bush camps (see this chapter, Living in the bush), they often lived off the land — their main diet was eels, pukeko, wild duck, poroporo, puha, water cress, and tawhara in season. Sometimes they would be away for two weeks at a time.

If the going got tough, the offsider rode his horse in front when the team could not see which way to go in dense bush or to make sure the footing was solid when they were wading through water. Kawhi walked all the way, giving the bullocks individual attention — calling them by name and giving them a gentle scratch behind the ear or under the chin.

Kawhi also did seasonal log hauling for Pera Paraima when she cleared her family land regained after the Pakeha buyers had taken the main kauri timber off it (see Chapter 7,

From the first efforts made in 1820 by the *Dromedary*'s bullocks in the Whangaroa Harbour until the late 1940s, bullock teams played an essential part in hauling kauri logs out of the bush.

Making good). The local kauri had been large — up to two metres in diameter, yielding eight to ten cubic metres of timber. Prime Cooper says that one stump was big enough for a horse to stand on. But most of Pera Paraima's remaining timber was small logs, mostly matai and taraire, that could be used only for fencing or cut up for local timber.

By the late 1940s, the last of the Pipiwai–Motatau kauri was almost depleted. Only puriri, totara, and other native timbers were being harvested, but they too were getting scarce. Kawhi scaled back his bullock team as the logs became lighter, but the competing bulldozers were now hauling two logs at a time and at a faster rate to his one. After nineteen years of hard bush slogging, he reluctantly set free the last of his bullocks.

LIVING IN THE BUSH

Although the hours were long and the labour often hard, work in the kauri bush was never dull and the forest huts, where the men had only the song of birds for music, and only the companionship of their mates for entertainment, were the setting for a very rewarding kind of life.

(EIGHTY-YEAR-OLD BUSHMAN, W. A. BELL 1965)

Bush cooks prepared hearty meals, bread, and baked goods in camp ovens and iron pots over an open fire. Clothes were hung to dry around the sides of the fireplace.

The only furniture in a bush shanty was double tiers of bunks (sacks spread over lengths of the springy climbing fern mange-mange served as mattresses), a large table and benches, and a kauri butcher's block at the fireplace end where the cook served the meals. Sometimes women took on this all-important job. Slaving long hours over a hot fire seven days a week was not child's play. Marjorie Clotworthy says:

I couldn't lift the big boilers and the camp ovens if I filled them with food, so my husband, before he went to work, would hang all the big heavy utensils on these hooks [above the fire] and I would fill them as I wanted to cook the tea . . .

(MACKAY 1991)

Short-sleeved flannel shirts were standard wear, with a second one worn over the top on damp days. Never washed, the smoke-impregnated stiffened flannel of this second shirt became waterproof:

> *Bushmen did not like buttons or wearing anything rough, so they generally persuaded some woman to crochet down the front opening of the shirts and over the armhole seams — this was much more comfortable.*
>
> (Bell 1965)

Although many kauri bushmen had a deserved reputation for being hard drinkers when they hit the town, alcohol was not permitted in the bush camps. These men are playing cards in the bush shanty at the main camp in the Kauaeranga in 1922. Sunday was a day of rest, but bushmen spent some of the day washing clothes and maintaining their tools. Sometimes, after finishing work on Saturday, they would walk out to the nearest town for a dance or night at the pub, followed by a football game on the Sunday.

Delivered each week with the stores, the ubiquitous *Auckland Weekly News* kept isolated bushmen in touch with the wider world, its local stories and photographs of the kauri industry confirming their place in it. Well-thumbed torn-up copies then served an equally vital role in the communal long-drop. As Jack Murray says:

> *The* Sporting Dramatic *was a shiny paper and not popular in the toilets.*
>
> (Mackay 1991)

Charismatic Joe Julian with half a blow to go in the fourteen-inch chop. One of the great New Zealand axe champions, Northland's Joe Julian won numerous national competitions from the 1940s until the 1960s. He was one of many kauri bushmen who took up the sport of wood-chopping. Although expertise with an axe had always been an essential part of the New Zealand and Australian colonial scene, chopping as a sport — founded in 1870 in Tasmania — was not recorded until 1888 in New Zealand. Modern competitive wood-chopping owes much to the skills of the best bushmen of the first few decades of the twentieth century. Other Northland names from the kauri days, like Jack Murray, Bert Collins, and Mick Griffin, also feature prominently in the record books.

Sharing isolation and long hours, hardship and danger, competition and camaraderie created a particular breed of tough capable men. Adept at turning their hands and skills to any task required of them, many of the bushmen of the early twentieth century became first-rate soldiers in two world wars. The reputation of the kauri bushmen, and its documentation in the widely read *Auckland Weekly News*, contributed to the development of the perceived rugged New Zealand colonial identity and character.

CHAPTER 9

Turn of the tide

RISE OF THE CONSERVATION MOVEMENT

On the turn

On the far side of the stream, tall columns of mature kauri cluster along the ridge, lifting their intermingling canopies well above the forest below. The track weaves through tree ferns and dense undergrowth, gradually climbing up onto the narrow ridge. There, the grave grey trunks of the mature kauri tower above the forest visitor. Wherever the eye alights — close by and through the bush on the other side of the valley — there are more trunks. Here, in this kauri grove, perhaps more than anywhere else in the kauri region, people can easily experience something of the awe-inspiring majesty of kauri in their prime. These kauri are the most accessible mature stand on the Coromandel, only a short walk in the Waiau Valley, a few kilometres south of Coromandel town. That such superb trees — 400–700 years old — escaped logging in easy terrain close to the sea is both a miracle and a mystery.

Inexplicably left untouched in the main timber sweep through the area in the late nineteenth century — perhaps because gold-mining took precedence locally over logging — the Waiau kauri grove was then scheduled for harvesting at the beginning of the Second

Damage caused by selective logging in Waipoua Forest during the Second World War, like this scene in the Kahuroa clearing, triggered Professor McGregor's conservation campaign and the formation of the Waipoua Forest Sanctuary in 1952.

World War. But bushmen contracted for the work decided otherwise. By that time, the stand's survival against the odds had given it a special status. At a bushmen's gathering in the local Coromandel hotel, indignation and beer flowed freely. Determined that the trees should continue to be conserved, the bushmen sent off a telegram of protest to the relevant government department in Wellington. The publicity that ensued resulted in the preservation and formal protection of the stand.

This first successful upwelling of public opinion against the logging of kauri was to be followed in the late 1940s and early 1950s by the high-profile efforts of Professor W. R. McGregor, one-time ecologist at Waipoua and then professor of zoology at the University of Auckland. Selective logging in Waipoua Forest, also initiated to satisfy wartime shipbuilding requirements, had continued beyond the end of the war. McGregor's passion and eloquent prose, backed by the efforts of the Waipoua Preservation Society, which he established, created the first nationwide conservation campaign in New Zealand:

> *What we seek to preserve in Waipoua is a gem with many facets: a fragment of old New Zealand, untamed in all its pristine glory; a remnant of an incredibly ancient garden of Nature, in all its inspiring loveliness and set in the midst of a vast dim-aisled cathedral that entombs an eternal silence.*
>
> (Halkett and Sale 1986)

The support of the press and petitions signed by thousands of people resulted in victory over parliament and policy. In 1952, Waipoua's kauri were protected by the formation of the Waipoua Forest Sanctuary.

Both these conservation successes had their beginnings nearly ninety years earlier — the first concerns about kauri forests and their inhabitants had emerged from the 1860s onwards.

Continuity and conservation

As early as 1863, the Austrian geologist Ferdinand von Hochstetter had warned that the rate of cutting would lead to kauri's extinction. His warning was followed by Premier Sir Julius Vogel's attempts in the mid-1870s to legislate against the wholesale destruction of all native forests. These attempts failed in the face of conflicting pressure to provide cleared land for increasing numbers of immigrants and timber for nationwide railway development — both also Vogel initiatives. In the north, the government continued to sell large blocks of kauri forest to sawmillers at fire-sale prices — fires frequently accompanied logging, gum-digging, and land clearance. Some figures suggest that more than half the kauri forests were burnt during land clearances that extended into the twentieth century. With the high

Destruction of large areas of forest by logging, fires, and land clearance, the resulting degradation of the land (like this denuded tract at Waipoua), and accompanying loss of native birds led to the establishment of many reserves by the beginning of the twentieth century.

percentage of logs already lost in failed recovery, the wastage was enormous.

Not until the late 1890s did concern about the long-term future of the forests lead to signs of real political change. Although the concern was mainly about sustaining the continuity of the colony's timber resource, the fate of the forests themselves also featured. After George Perrin (an Australian conservator of forests) wrote a strongly worded government-commissioned report in 1897 on the parlous state of New Zealand's forests, attempts were at last made to survey what kauri resource remained, reserve some of the forests, and plan sustainable-yield management of the rest. Attention also turned to planting an alternative resource of exotic timber species. Perversely, the rate of cutting kauri accelerated — 1906 was the peak year of production.

Protection and preservation

At the same time, people were realising that the value of native forests extended far beyond timber. Accelerated erosion was already stripping soil from unstable hill country denuded of its forest cover. By the 1870s, New Zealand's spectacular scenery was attracting visitors, encouraging a drive led by ex-Premier and explorer/artist William Fox to set aside scenic reserves and national parks, along the lines of the newly established Yellowstone National

Park in America. By the 1880s, scientists and gentlemen-naturalists such as Thomas Potts were becoming alarmed by the demise of native bird-life, depleted by forest clearance, introduced predators — rats, cats, stoats, ferrets, and weasels — and the activities of the Austrian naturalist/collector Andreas Reischek.

In response, the government had given reserve status of various sorts to hundreds of thousands of hectares by the beginning of the twentieth century. As a result of the efforts of far-sighted conservationists such as Harry Ell, many large remote areas were indeed preserved for the protection of flora and fauna or for their scenic values, some later becoming national parks. However, the creation of reserves did not gather pace until most usable land had already been exploited — by definition, reserved land could have no value for settlement or agriculture. What is more, forest reserve status often meant 'reserved for future use' — this certainly applied to kauri forests like Waipoua.

War over Waipoua

Purchased from rival but related chiefs Tiopira Kinaki (Te Roroa) and Parore Te Awha (Nga Puhi) in 1876, Waipoua Forest was initially destined for clearing and settling. But the forest escaped any logging until the twentieth century because of a verbal agreement with Parore to protect the forest long-term for the benefit of both Maori and Pakeha, and — more pragmatically — because of its isolation. Ironically, it was the increasing and conflicting concerns about preserving the kauri resource that swivelled the spotlight onto Waipoua.

Waipoua had been reserved as a state forest in 1906. But the forest came under increasing pressure as the kauri resource diminished elsewhere. Despite botanist Leonard Cockayne's recognition of Waipoua's ecological status as the largest surviving example of ancient kauri forest, and its legal status as a protected reserve — let alone any tacit agreement with the original Maori owners — the politicians reverted to the original intention of logging most of the forest. At one stage, a mere eighty hectares was seen as sufficient for a proposed kauri national park.

The First World War intervened, but in the 1920s Waipoua Forest became the focus of early management efforts by the newly formed State Forest Service. The latest scientific research suggested that the best way to ensure kauri's continuing presence would be to remove mature and aging trees, creating light 'wells' in which a new generation could start to grow. Forests tended according to best European silvicultural practice could neatly resolve the conflicting goals of conservation of kauri and — by harvesting valuable timber before aging trees deteriorated — continuity of timber supplies.

Selective logging of old kauri began in outlying blocks. A research station and kauri nursery were set up. The government bought up adjacent blocks in the Waipoua Native Reserve — owned and lived on by Te Roroa — for establishing pine plantations. Then

Kaipara's Gordon Coates, long-time advocate of local economic development and now Prime Minister, promoted the building of a road plumb through the middle of the forest — arousing much public suspicion about necessity and intent. The now-famous road through Waipoua was completed in 1928. It not only opened up the intended access to the Hokianga, it also opened up access for active management of the forest.

After the hiatus of the 1930s Depression, the Forest Service dreams of a well-managed kauri forest at Waipoua were reactivated with the judicious removal of some dead trees in 1941. But the renewed timber demands of the Second World War soon accelerated the amount of selective logging. Not only dead standing kauri but also healthy living trees began falling to the cross saws.

By now, some of those involved in the fledgling conservation movement were expressing revulsion against any further logging of what little native forest remained after a century of destructive clear-felling. Waipoua became the battleground for two opposing philosophies. Nature knows best (non-interference to ensure preservation) versus man knows better (silvicultural management to ensure regeneration). New, well-organised groups such as the Royal Forest and Bird Protection Society and the Waipoua Preservation Society — led by Professor McGregor — lined up against the Forest Service. The persuasive McGregor did not hesitate in lambasting the Forest Service and what he considered its dastardly plan to log this last remnant of primeval kauri forest. With both sides of the philosophical argument convinced of their ground, opinions became polarised.

Professor McGregor and the conservationists began pushing for the whole of Waipoua to be redesignated as a national park — removing it from Forest Service management. In 1952, over 9000 hectares of Waipoua were preserved for all time as a Forest Sanctuary by parliamentary proclamation. Although this fell short of national park status — and the care of Waipoua remained with the Forest Service — the Sanctuary had its own legally established Advisory Committee. The war over Waipoua had largely been won.

But like the end of many wars, this much-hailed outcome contained the seeds of

Left Cars carrying the official guests travel through Waipoua Forest on the new road for the ceremonial opening in 1928.

Above Professor W. R. McGregor, leader of the campaign to preserve Waipoua Forest.

The kauri nursery at Waipoua raised thousands of kauri seedlings as part of the New Zealand Forest Service's silvicultural policy of actively managing the remaining kauri forests.

future strife. Neither side had yielded in its convictions about the best way to ensure the future of kauri forests. Conflicts over management of not only kauri but all native forests were to continue. The polarisation of the Forest Service and the conservation movement hardened, with consequences that have continued into the twenty-first century (see Chapter 10, Present obligations, future opportunities). It was perhaps this polarisation that resulted in the overlooking of another significant faction in the fight for Waipoua — the Te Roroa tribe.

Already at odds with government and the Forest Service over the encroachment of logging and pine planting onto land that contained burial places, Te Roroa had actively opposed both the felling of kauri and the building of the road. But despite their obvious interests, Te Roroa were not offered a place on the all-important Advisory Committee for the newly formed Forest Sanctuary. This omission seems surprising. Other North Island Maori tribes had already been actively involved in the formation of New Zealand's first scenic reserves and national parks. Most notable was Tuwharetoa chief Te Heuheu's gifting of the sacred mountains Tongariro, Ngauruhoe, and Ruapehu to the people of New Zealand in 1887. This gift had formed the nucleus of the country's first national park — Tongariro (gazetted in 1909). As a means of pre-empting the potential division and sale of disputed land and preserving the mana of Tuwharetoa, Te Heuheu's gesture was masterful. To this day, Tuwharetoa retains representation on all the park's administrative boards. The slight to Te Roroa over the management of the Waipoua Sanctuary was therefore considerable. The repercussions would later compound those already caused by the rift between Forest Service and conservationists (see Chapter 10, Cultural collisions).

The ebbing tide

Even before the fight for Waipoua, cultural shifts in the perception of kauri's intrinsic value were taking place among Maori as well as Pakeha. Nowhere were these more evident than in some small Maori communities, where reaction against the continued loss of the forests was causing a return to the value kauri had held in the past. This shift contributed to the renaissance of traditional uses of Tane Mahuta's magnificent trees (see this chapter, Community, commemoration, and culture).

Although the saving of Waipoua in 1952 was a major milestone, battles over the management of the remaining kauri forests were to continue. The quantity of kauri timber extracted from state forests plummeted, but this was only partly the result of regulation and raised consciousness. Kauri timber was now in high demand, but most of the available resource in both private and state forests had already been logged. Salvage and selective logging of kauri to meet contractual obligations was to continue in state forests until 1985. Logging operations in each forest were targeted in turn by conservationists and protesters, building on the tactics and success of the Waipoua campaign.

These continuing clashes between the Forest Service, timber interests, and the strengthening conservation movement were to reveal a gradual shift in focus from the trees themselves to perceptions of the intrinsic value of forest as habitat for wildlife. It was this shift that finally achieved the halt to logging of live kauri in state forests. And it was this shift that led to the restructuring of some key government departments soon afterwards, in 1987.

Changing currents at Coromandel

With Waipoua out of bounds, salvage operations continued through the 1960s and 1970s in the Coromandel forests. Powerful tractors were used to winch chainsaw-felled dead or dying kauri from precipitous pinnacles that had been out of the reach of the earlier bushmen. Many of these trees had been killed by the indiscriminate fires that had swept the Coromandel during and after logging. Some trees were dying after being bled — equally indiscriminately — for gum. Only one percent of the Coromandel forests had survived the main era of the kauri industry intact.

Salvaging dead trees did not make participating bushman and manager of the Thames Sawmilling Company, Rei Hamon, uncomfortable — but the occasional felling of healthy trees did. In 1961, he supervised the felling of a large healthy kauri from the watershed high above Tapu. Containing thirty-four cubic metres of usable heart timber, the log was too large for transport by road. He explains:

> *When that tree fell, it had been standing there for maybe a thousand years in its healthy growth. When it came down, the cross-cutters and I had the job of getting it down the hill at Tapu and into the sea — it was the last kauri log to be floated across the Hauraki Gulf to Auckland. I went back later to where it had been standing, and there were birds fluttering around there, kaka and kereru, that had nested in that tree for generations. That was the finish. I handed in my resignation. I vowed never to fell another healthy tree.*

Ten years later, Rei Hamon led efforts to stop renewed logging on the Coromandel. Having turned to art after a fall from a horse ended his active days in 1966, he was already earning a nationwide reputation for his portrayals of New Zealand bush. Rei used this profile to gain publicity for growing pressure to preserve the mature stands of kauri in the rugged Manaia block, which had been gridded for felling. His successful search for some surviving giant kauri contributed to the area being declared a Forest Sanctuary in 1972.

Wrecked on the rocks at Warawara

Despite the growing icon status of aging giant kauri and the increasing support for the preservation of all remaining kauri forest, conflicting economic pressures continued to sway government policy-makers. In 1967 — after pressure from the Hokianga County Council to provide much-needed employment opportunities — a government tender to fell timber in Warawara Forest (north of the Hokianga Harbour) was won by Whitecliffs Sawmilling Company. Isolation and inaccessibility had previously protected this forest from systematic logging, but its mature kauri had suffered from the depredations of gum-bleeders. Stands containing large percentages of dead or dying old kauri on Warawara's steep plateau were targeted. The more than 56,000 cubic metres of timber contracted for extraction over the next ten years included these dying kauri.

Strict controls were to be imposed. Only kauri selected and marked by the Forest Service could be felled, the logging operation was to avoid excessive soil disturbance or damage to healthy young trees, and the work was to be monitored by the Forest Service.

Public outrage at clearfelling, wastage, and destruction of kauri saplings and seedlings at Warawara Forest, despite the controls imposed, achieved an abrupt halt to kauri logging in the forest in 1974.

Despite these controls, the use of heavy machinery to create access roads and extract kauri in often steep terrain soon reduced logged areas to scarred battlefields. Abandoned logs and tree heads, crushed saplings, and trampled seedlings lay heaped amid churned mud. The company also felled healthy mature kauri. The Forest Service failed dismally to prevent such wastage of valuable timber and devastation of the forest environment. Its failure provoked public outrage.

Publicity and protest brought an abrupt halt to all logging in Warawara Forest in 1974. As an advertisement for sustained-yield management of virgin stands of mature kauri, Warawara was a disaster. Attempting reparation, the Forest Service eventually achieved the preservation of the remaining forest containing kauri as a Forest Sanctuary in 1979, with an adjoining ecological area preserved in 1982. But it was too late. The Forest Service continued to be haunted by the shame of Warawara — a useful weapon in the hands of the conservation movement.

On the wings of song

In the 1970s, Puketi Forest (inland Bay of Islands) became the main source of selectively logged kauri from state forests. At the same time, the allowable cut of mature kauri was dramatically reduced and ecological principles were used to select trees for logging. Contracted to Lane and Sons at Totara North, the last of the mainstream loggers in state forests was local bushman Gil Whitaker, from Moerewa. Over the next ten years, he removed marked trees from an area of about 100 hectares to provide high-quality timber milled at Lane and Sons for boat-building. John Beachman, at that time an Environmental Ranger for the Forest Service, had the unenviable task of selecting and marking the Puketi trees, based on an earlier inventory:

> *By 1979, I'd mapped all the stands from aerial photographs, and that was showing that the harvest simply wasn't sustainable. The kauri trees just weren't there. It would have fallen over by itself before much longer. . . . The logging of mature forest is ultimately self-defeating. It started looking more and more absurd.*

But in the end what 'chased the Forest Service out of Puketi' was the presence of kokako. Activist and conservationist Stephen King — fresh from a successful tree-top protest that had stopped logging in Pureora Forest (west of Lake Taupo), a main refuge for kokako — involved the Wildlife Service in a search for the endangered bird in Puketi in 1979 and 1983. These surveys revealed a breeding population of 100 kokako. One of the largest populations in the country, the birds were most common in parts of the forest that had been

The discovery of the largest remaining population of endangered kokako at Puketi Forest in 1979 heralded the halt to all logging of living kauri in state forests by 1981.

undisturbed. To conservationist glee, kokako actively avoided logged stands. The birds favoured the outer branches of ridge-top mature kauri as singing posts during the all-important breeding season. Logging removed their singing trees and disrupted the canopy and understorey in which they fed. Rare birds won over luxury boats. Logging was permanently halted at Puketi after 1979. But Lane and Sons, specialists in kauri for boat-building since the early twentieth century, were then forced to pay top prices to farmers for living kauri off private land. Trees that would otherwise have been preserved fell to the chainsaws until the demand for green kauri for boats began to fade after the mid-1990s.

Shifting shoals

Disasters like Warawara and the continued conspicuous felling of mature kauri had detracted from other more benign Forest Service initiatives. By the 1980s, improved knowledge of kauri growth and ecology formed the basis for extensive attempts to establish plantations of kauri in previously logged areas of state forests. Hundreds of thousands of kauri seedlings raised at the Forest Service nursery at Sweetwater (near Kaitaia) had been planted out in Northland, on the Coromandel, and near Katikati. Further areas of

This healthy silviculturally managed kauri stand in Russell Forest, here ninety years old in 1975, had been thinned in 1962.

The Bergman brothers of Northland Kauri, Oromahoe, flew this portable mill into state forests like Puketi to salvage abandoned kauri heads and logs uncovered when the Forest Service was clearing second-generation radiata pine. Chris Bergman recalls: 'At Puketi we pulled 1000 cubic metres of kauri logs — all salvage — from one block. It kept us going for about three years, cutting it for furniture and turning.'

untouched kauri stands had been set aside as reserves, and extensive areas of regenerating 'second-crop' kauri had been added to the forest estate. Many tracks, picnic areas, and campsites had been developed for public recreation as part of the new multi-use policy adopted by the Forest Service for state forests.

In 1981, the last mature kauri logged by the Forest Service were taken from Herekino Forest (north of the Hokianga), to fulfil final contractual obligations to Lane and Sons. The focus then moved to Russell Forest (south of the Bay of Islands). Acquired as a kauri management area in the 1950s and 1960s, the young stands of rickers had been actively thinned. In 1980, helicopters were used experimentally to extract logs from Russell Forest. John Beachman recalls: 'The choppers we were using could lift about a cubic metre at a time. That was interesting, intricate work.'

Above While prices and demand for kauri remained high during the 1990s, green and salvage logging continued on private land. In 1991, the Bergman brothers felled the Balderston kauri at Kaiwaka, a large tree that had been killed by lightning in 1986.

Left The Balderston kauri begins its fall until the last fibres tear and the tree falls to the ground.

Below The brothers stand on the stump of the fallen giant.

By the mid-1980s, only old kauri heads and stumps salvaged from previously logged areas were coming out of the state forests. Innovative loggers like Warwick Davies and brothers Chris and Ari Bergman were now using helicopters to take portable sawmills into the forest and to lift out salvaged kauri logs, substantially reducing the amount of environmental damage.

Forest Service management policy for the kauri forests now indicated a major shift to preservation of the remaining forests as natural ecosystems, with associated pest-management plans for protecting their distinctive plants and wildlife. Kauri forests in Northland and the Coromandel became grouped under the protection of multi-purpose forest parks. But plans for continued active management of second-crop kauri as future production areas were not well received by the still antagonistic conservation movement. Ring-barking or felling of competing understorey native trees in an unproved bid to accelerate kauri growth — dying trees the highly visible result — were seen as anathema in a natural environment. The Forest Service's clearance and planting of pines on substantial tracts of northern scrubland and marginal farmland, that left undisturbed might revert to kauri, merely confirmed the perceived conflict of interests.

In 1987, the conservation movement celebrated its long sought-after separation of the Forest Service's conflicting roles of preservation and production. All government agencies that had responsibilities for management of Crown land were disbanded — the Forest Service, the Wildlife Service, and the Department of Lands and Survey. A new Department of Conservation was established, dedicated to managing and protecting all native flora and fauna — and the reserves, forest parks, and national parks in which they lived. At the same time, the newly formed Native Forest Restoration Trust had achieved additions to the Waipoua Forest Sanctuary. Conservation groups like Forest and Bird began pushing for a Kauri National Park in Northland that would place the kauri forest remnants under greater protection. The future of the kauri forests and their precious inhabitants had never looked brighter.

COMMUNITY, COMMEMORATION, AND CULTURE

Although until the 1940s, the kauri timber and gum industries had provided much-needed employment for the rural Maori communities of the north, some Maori land-owners were now making efforts to protect their remaining mature kauri. At Motatau, Pera Paraima cleared only the areas that had already been logged on the family land she had bought back (see Chapter 8, The last of the obsolete cowboys). Family anecdotes report her fury when son Sam Prime cut some of the remaining large kauri. Kevin Prime recalls:

> *My grandmother always said you shouldn't take anything for personal use that you had not planted. . . . If you didn't plant the kauri trees, you shouldn't touch them. It was like water — they belonged to everybody.*

In 1933, with the centenary of the Treaty of Waitangi approaching, it was to Pera Paraima that now-prominent political leaders Sir Apirana Ngata (Ngati Porou) and Tau Henare (Ngati Hine) came for the timber needed to build a commemorative meeting house at Waitangi. That year, Governor-General Lord Bledisloe had bought the dilapidated Treaty House with its grounds and gifted them to the nation. The National Trust set up to restore and administer the house included representatives of the main northern chiefs. Among them was Tau Henare — who provided kauri shingles from the family sawmill at Motatau for re-roofing the house.

Renewed interest in the Waitangi site coincided with a drive to build carved meeting houses, churches, and halls in Maori communities as a way of maintaining traditional values — part of Sir Apirana Ngata's land development schemes of the 1930s. When the first major celebrations were held at Waitangi in 1934, Maori from all over the North Island were present to attend the laying of the foundation stone for a fully carved Whare Runanga. This meeting house was to represent all tribes of New Zealand and symbolise the relationship between Pakeha and Maori signified by the 1840 Treaty of Waitangi.

In response to the request for timber to build this house, Pera Paraima did not hesitate. According to Kevin Prime:

> *She got her sons and the workers to cut the trees down — kauri and totara. They pit-sawed all the timber and they took it down to the Motatau marae — that's where the carvings were done. The carvings were done by carvers*

The interior of the meeting house at Waitangi, carved out of timber from Motatau.

from all over the country, but all the timber came from Motatau. My grandmother gave that timber, not only gave it, but did so willingly, because it was for that wider purpose.

Also a commemorative project — initiated by Te Puea Herangi, leader of Tainui and the joint work of Waikato and Nga Puhi tribes — was the building of the thirty-five-metre-long Waitangi war canoe (named *Nga-toki-matawhao-rua* after Kupe's original canoe). Two large kauri were felled in Puketi Forest for this canoe. The tree for the main central section was three metres in diameter. Its felling took five Nga Puhi bushmen five hours of solid work with axe and cross-cut saw. Years later, Taupuhi Eruera, one of the tree fellers and carvers (from Utakura, near Lake Omapere) told Hec Busby about the felling. He recalls:

The tree for the middle section stood for three days after it was cut — sat on its stump. I think Taupuhi eventually climbed up into the head of the tree somehow, to attach the rope, and the bullocks pulled the tree over.

The canoe was an immense undertaking. Three months were spent on preliminary adzing before the twenty-one-metre-long log was dragged out of the steep forest terrain by a team of twenty-four bullocks — a journey that took three weeks. Only then did modern machinery

The completed canoe, *Nga-toki-matawhao-rua* (on the right), rests at Waitangi.

transport the log to the Kerikeri Inlet for three months' immersion in brackish water. A second tree was felled for the bow and stern sections, a third (from Tutamoe) for topstrake planks to heighten the freeboard of the hull. The carvers took twenty-seven months to complete the work under the guidance of Piri Poutapu (Waikato). The felling, shaping, and carving of this magnificent canoe were accompanied by traditional protocol and ritual, in keeping with the significance of the project.

One of the two kauri felled in Puketi Forest to build *Nga-toki-matawhao-rua* here barked and scarfed. Its trunk was over five metres in girth and twenty metres in height to the first branch.

These major representations of traditional Maori skills at Waitangi were the first time for several generations that kauri had been used for the purposes for which Maori had once reserved it. The construction of the Whare Runanga and the great canoe, the coming together of several tribes for the work, and the conspicuous Maori presence on the Waitangi site reflected a subtle change in both Maori and Pakeha relationships. This change had its roots in the Maori participation in two world wars — gaining new Pakeha respect — and the growing confidence of new-style Maori leaders in using the political system to gain improvements for their people.

Chapter 10

Habitat and heritage

Into the twenty-first century

Encounters of the third kind

The first rays of the sun tip the kauri crowns on Canoe Ridge. Beyond, still in darkness, other kauri line ridges rising above the early mist. A few kaka fly noisily across the landscape. The rapid-fire chatter of parakeets contrasts with the sleepy mumble of kukupa. Other birds call, swelling the dawn chorus. But their voices are mostly those of immigrants — rosellas and mynahs, magpies and blackbirds. The deep bell-like chimes of the kokako are rarely heard. This is Puketi Forest in 2000. Since 1983, the biggest population of kokako known has dwindled to seven or eight birds. None of them is female. Despite kokako saving Puketi from further logging, preserving the forest has not saved kokako.

In 1983, warning signs were already emerging. The status of the kokako population was unknown, but fewer than half the birds seemed to be paired — and not all of those attempted to nest each year. No one knew whether this was normal, but it seems likely that Puketi's kokako were already under pressure. Possums had arrived at Puketi by the mid-1970s, and had now spread throughout the forest. Some of the understorey food plants favoured by kokako were already succumbing to over-indulgence by possums. Suspicion that possums ate kokako fledglings for 'afters' was being confirmed by research elsewhere. Other known predators of kokako were present in the forest — ship rats, stoats, and ferrets.

Within the decade, the Department of Conservation was intensively controlling possums in Puketi, and the vegetation recovered sufficiently to ensure food supplies for kokako. Translocated fledglings from Mataraua Forest (inland from Waipoua) were then brought in. But it was too late. John Beachman, continuing his long association with Puketi as Area Manager for the Department of Conservation at Kerikeri, explains:

> *The Department has made big efforts to save kokako in Puketi, but we haven't got enough birds to work with. Birds raised artificially or brought in as fledglings don't behave normally — they hear bird calls wrong. The problem is that young translocated kokako moved out of the protected areas.*

With the Mataraua population not robust enough for continued cropping, the Department is now pairing artificially raised Northland chicks with female chicks from Auckland's Tiritiri Matangi Island. These pairs are housed at Auckland and Hamilton Zoos. Any progeny will be shifted to a safe offshore island until the translocation difficulties are solved.

The collapse of the kokako population at Puketi is but one of many problems faced by the Department of Conservation in Northland. As a signatory to the international 1993 Convention on Biological Diversity, New Zealand is required to work towards conserving national biodiversity (all living organisms and their ecosystems), both for its intrinsic values and for any potential future benefits for humankind. As part of this requirement, for kauri forests alone the Department has recovery plans for other threatened species and has to manage pests and weeds, fire control, and visitor impacts — major priorities that need to be dealt with across a fragmented forest landscape and with limited resources. At the same time, the Department has to accommodate the sometimes conflicting agendas of local Maori, conservation groups, tourism promoters, and local community interests. This Department combating 'sinister forces in the habitat' is itself often under siege.

Sinister forces

Although the removal of kauri in state forests from the threat of logging and the creation of a Department of Conservation had been major victories for the conservation movement, it soon became clear that nature could not be left to do the nurturing. Degraded kauri forests were being invaded by exotic animal and plant pests. Their impact probably rivalled any threat to intrinsic ecosystem values posed by selective logging.

Ill-conceived introductions of exotic animals by colonists had continued into the

As a signatory to many international conventions on the need to preserve biological biodiversity and the quality of soil and water resources for the use of future generations, New Zealand has major obligations to protect the environment. This pristine scene in Waima Forest, in the Hokianga, was photographed above the intake for Rawene's water supply.

twentieth century, despite the warnings of the more enlightened. As a result, many of New Zealand's endemic plants and animals — which had evolved in isolation without browsers (other than moa) or predatory mammals — were under threat. Invading deer, goats, and possums rampaged through the forests like soccer hooligans on package tours until the best of the food supplies ran out. Some native inhabitants were forced to move out, and those that stayed put were subjected to the predatory intentions of the invaders as well as competition from them for the remaining food supplies.

In the north, some of the invaders were late-comers. The build-up of possums in the kauri forests roughly coincided with the transfer of responsibilities from the Forest Service to the new Department of Conservation. Within a few years, inhabitants and habitats in forests like Puketi and Waipoua were facing major threats to their future. Unlike soccer hooligans, who can be put on the next plane home, pests such as possums and goats are here to stay. In 1990, with the support of the Native Forest Restoration Trust, the Department sowed 100 tonnes of 1080 bait across 17,000 hectares of kauri forest at Waipoua — the largest aerial poisoning campaign ever conducted. The number of possums killed — a massive 200,000 (twelve per hectare, with five per hectare considered dense) — indicated the scale of the problem.

If selective logging of native forests was the issue that polarised conservationist and Forest Service opinion in the 1980s, the use of 1080 has equally polarised opinion since the early 1990s. In the past decade, the Department of Conservation has come up against increasing public resistance to aerial spraying of 1080 — arguably the most effective biodegradable poison available and the most effective present option for controlling possums in remote forests. Public resistance ranges from perceived impacts on the native inhabitants and potential contamination of waterways, to lack of consultation and opportunities lost for employing local Maori as possum trappers. Long term, it seems likely that the only effective way of permanently reducing possum numbers would be to use biological control technology. Research is showing that a potentially successful and humane approach would be to spread genetically induced infertility through the population, steadily lowering the birth rate. But the use of such genetically modified organisms (GMOs) is already shaping up to be a major conservation issue of the twenty-first century.

To the casual eye, less conspicuous than the damage caused by animal pests — but with potentially devastating consequences — is the inexorable spread of weeds into native forests. The number of exotic plant species now growing in New Zealand is far greater than the number of native species. Nationwide, the ongoing spread of weeds from agriculture, forestry, and horticulture is threatening biodiversity in many natural habitats. In the north, the weed problem is at explosion point. Kauri forests are particularly vulnerable because the warm moist northern climate favours weed spread. Over 100 weed species now threaten native habitats in Northland. From Auckland City alone, four new plant species 'escape' into the wild each year.

Full-scale pest and weed control is expensive, labour-intensive, and dependent on long-term commitment — from both practitioners and the politicians holding the purse strings. Even if pests are successfully controlled, competition from naturalised exotic grasses and other introduced weeds can prevent or slow the establishment of early successional natives

Left The scrub communities characteristic of Northland's gum-lands support many unusual plant species, including orchids not found anywhere else. Adapted to the acidic peat soils, many of these orchids, like this blue-flowered species, are now threatened by large-scale loss of habitat caused by draining and pasture conversion.

Top Fragrant mairehau with its pure white flowers is a characteristic kauri shrub companion that, like kauri, does not naturally grow south of a line running from Kawhia Harbour in the west to Katikati and the Kaimai Range in the east.

Above The world's tallest moss, New Zealand's 'giant moss' flourishes in the kauri forests of the north, where it can be seen on the road edge in Waipoua Forest.

This tranquil scene shows the Kaihu River at Trounson Kauri Park. A 450-hectare forest reserve near Waipoua, this park is managed as a Department of Conservation Mainland Island and contains one of the best and most accessible stands of kauri in the north. Intensive management of pests began in the park in 1995, aimed at rodents, possums, stoats and ferrets, and feral cats. Numbers of kukupa have now increased, the park is thought to be one of the best breeding sites for North Island brown kiwi. North Island robins have also now been successfully re-introduced.

like manuka and kanuka in areas where forest restoration is being attempted. Re-introduced native birds face continuing competition from aggressive and ubiquitous entrenched exotic birds like magpies, mynahs, and rosellas. In complex forests like those of the north, throwing the book at each and every invader — and continuing to do so — may be the only option. This option is showcased by the Department of Conservation in a Mainland Island project at Trounson Kauri Park (south of Waipoua Forest), where pest control is intensive and ongoing.

Efforts to restore native forests by removing pests and weeds may never reach their desired goals — some of the impacts may be irreversible. Interactions between invaders and natural forest dynamics can change composition and structure, eventually altering the direction or pace of long-term forest succession. Goals for restoration that accept an ongoing degree of alteration to both forests and their inhabitants may ultimately have a greater chance of success.

Cultural collisions

When all the kauri forests and reserves scattered throughout Northland came under the jurisdiction of the Department of Conservation in 1987, Forest and Bird mounted a campaign for a fourteenth national park to at last represent New Zealand's subtropical flora and fauna. Gordon Ell, one-time National President of Forest and Bird and articulate advocate for a Northland Kauri National Park, created an innovative concept that linked the natural landscapes formed by fragmented kauri 'islands' on ridges and plateaus with the cultural landscapes of the intervening farmed valleys. After initial investigations that followed the process dictated by the National Parks Act 1980, the public was asked to respond to the proposal in 1990. The public response, mostly from Forest and Bird supporters and recreational groups, was enthusiastic. The response from northern Maori tribes, however, was not.

The northern tribes were unanimous that any such proposal must be put on hold until all relevant Treaty of Waitangi claims had been resolved — affecting most of the land involved. The 1992 Waitangi Tribunal report on the 127-year-old Te Roroa claim had just been released, recommending that some of the disputed Waipoua lands be returned to the tribe. But it was to be another thirteen years before a Deed of Settlement was signed between the Crown and Te Roroa – late in 2005, and the associated still-debated Claim Settlement Bill has yet to pass through parliament two years later.

In the meantime, outstanding Treaty claims aside, the National Parks Act process — and the newly formed New Zealand Conservation Authority's interpretation of it — fell far short of Maori expectations of being fully included in any decisions on policy and management of the kauri forests. With their input not sought until after the proposal had

Over the years, repeated grading of the narrow road through Waipoua damaged adjacent kauri trees. In 1995, Transit New Zealand formed an unlikely but successful partnership with activist and Waipoua protector Stephen King to design their forthcoming upgrade of the road. By adopting Stephen's radical idea of building bridges over the root systems of the three most vulnerable kauri, Transit solved the earlier drainage and compaction problems. The health of the trees has since improved.

been formulated, the northern tribes felt they had been relegated to the status of 'just another interest group'.

The Conservation Authority formally acknowledged the significance of the Maori land claims and grievances and recognised that until they had all been resolved, a kauri national park could not proceed. But the Authority continued its own investigations until the mid 1990s. As Gordon Ell explains:

> *The Conservation Authority's responsibility was to complete the process of establishing scientifically that these areas had values that warranted protection under Section 8 of the Conservation Act as National Parks.*
>
> (COMMEMORATIVE ORAL HISTORIES FROM FOREST AND BIRD'S SEVENTY-FIFTH ANNIVERSARY)

What the Conservation Authority saw as a separate and legislatively mandated process of evaluating ecological, natural, and scenic criteria was seen by northern Maori as compounding the evidence that Treaty of Waitangi principles, partnership requirements, Maori status as traditional guardians of the forests, and Maori traditional rights were all being ignored.

As a result, the Authority's final elegant proposal for a more coherent national park framework based around the Hokianga forests was not well received by the northern tribes. For Te Roroa — the most directly affected tribe — the process exacerbated an already uneasy relationship with the Department of Conservation that was partly the result of earlier poor experiences with government agencies (see Chapter 9, War over Waipoua).

Today, although the proposal for a kauri national park may continue to sit on the back burner until all Treaty claims are resolved, Alex Nathan, Chairman of Te Roroa, says that their relationship with the Department of Conservation has improved significantly. The Deed of Settlement confers Tarehu status on those parts of Waipoua not being returned to the tribe, acknowledging Te Roroa's special association with the Forest. This status requires the Department to work closely with the tribe to formulate principles for their potential joint management of Waipoua. Although the Deed does not specifically cater for a kauri national park, its passage into law makes it more likely that such a park would gain the blessing of Te Roroa and the other northern Maori tribes.

Community, cooperation, and conservation

In recent years, a new form of conservation management has been emerging from the chrysalis of such conflict, but only partly because of a change in philosophy. Management needs often exceed the Department of Conservation's resources. As a result, conservation efforts increasingly rely on cooperation with non-government organisations like Forest and Bird, corporate sponsors, and local community trusts of various sorts, with the Department adopting a more strategic and advisory role.

Community groups are taking on pest and weed control, and associated species recovery, on land where the Department's resources do not stretch. For example, public interest in kiwi recovery at Kerikeri has now grown to forty active Northland Landcare groups that get biodiversity funding for shooting possums and trapping stoats. Local volunteers have revived the Department nursery to raise native trees for restoration projects. The Puketi Forest Trust launched in late 2003, which raises funds to help restore Puketi and eventually re-introduce kokako, is successfully gaining increases in kiwi numbers with an effective rat control campaign. In support of such efforts, the Department of Conservation runs workshops and provides advice, recognising that public participation in pest control is the best education. As John Beachman points out:

> *There are no self-managing habitats any more, so if you want to reinstate species, you have to do pest control. As people become actively involved in their local areas, they do seem to be picking up on that.*

Ngati Hine and kukupa recovery

Perhaps the template for later cooperative projects in Northland was a pest-control programme initiated by Ngati Hine in 1989. In the five years it took the government to hand back environmental management of 300-hectare Motatau Forest to the tribe, Ngati Hine went ahead with pest control — with the unofficial blessing of the Department of Conservation and its welcomed practical support. Initially set up as a government-funded residential training scheme, the project trained pest-control operators in the forest, getting rid of all the pests in the process.

In 1994 (the year the forest's management was formally handed back), Ngati Hine agreed to participate in a research project on restoring kukupa (New Zealand pigeons) with Landcare Research (a Crown Research Institute set up after further restructuring of government environmental research). In dealing with a once-again increasing possum population, scientific protocol and Maori pragmatism sometimes clashed. Kevin Prime gives an example:

> *We got our first evidence on video camera of a pigeon nest being predated by possums. The scientists wanted* twenty *nests predated before they'd accept the evidence. What nonsense!*

Compromise and goodwill prevailed. In 1996, after a year of scientific monitoring of the status of the forest and its pests, the possums were successfully poisoned. But kukupa nests monitored the following year showed continued predation. Possums were coming in from outside the forest. A meeting with neighbouring property owners, including pine-forest owner Carter Holt Harvey, led to cooperative possum control throughout a wide buffer zone. Kevin Prime explains:

> *After that, we monitored seven nests and got seven chicks fledged — all seven flew away. This was 100 percent success two years after the initial poisoning.*

With the bit between their teeth, Ngati Hine have continued their pest control efforts. Buying up privately owned blocks of native forest, they have doubled the area of local forest now being protected — gifting the land to the government. Work in Motatau Forest now includes kiwi protection after recent Department of Conservation counts revealed a large kiwi population, winning biodiversity funding for labour. Kevin Prime has become 'an evangelist for the cause', talking to Maori tribes throughout the north and other groups interested in setting up similar projects: 'We're aiming to make the whole of Taitokerau a pest-free zone.'

Although Ngati Hine's ultimate objective is to restore the kukupa population to levels where cultural harvest is once more sustainable, Kevin acknowledges that this is a long way off:

We're prepared to wait until kukupa are declared a pest by the local authority before we start eating them. When all the fruit farmers in Kerikeri are complaining about the pigeons coming and eating the kiwifruit, the guavas, the feijoas — that's when cultural harvest would be sustainable.

Bicultural cooperation at Waipoua

Early restoration work and land purchases at Waipoua by the Forest Restoration Trust have now been extended by a partnership with Te Roroa. In 1998, Stephen King and Alex Nathan (Chairman of Te Roroa) formed the Waipoua Forest Trust to give practical recognition to Te Roroa's traditional guardianship of the forest. Te Roroa share joint title on farmland bought with Lottery Grants Board funding to establish the Millennium Kauri Forest. Restoration is based on direct-sowing of manuka seed to form a protective cover in which kauri can be planted. This technique was successfully pioneered in the Professor McGregor Reserve, using adapted discing machinery. Te Roroa people collect all the manuka seed and do all the sowing. By the end of the 2004 planting season, over 800 million manuka seeds had been sown, and over 50,000 manuka seedlings and 6000 kauri seedlings had been planted. Stephen King raises all the kauri seedlings for the Millennium Kauri Forest, using seed from Tane Mahuta 'and the other big trees that were alive at the time of Christ'. Much of the maintenance work in the tree nursery is done by volunteers — mainly international backpackers with time to stay for several months.

As well as planting the new forest, Te Roroa people are now involved in predator trapping to protect the large kiwi population. Stephen King's wish to extend predator control throughout the kauri forests of the north parallels that of Ngati Hine — perhaps another opportunity for joint partnership. The Trust has also taken on a ten-year contract to maintain the vegetation along the road through Waipoua Forest, as Stephen explains:

We've got a war on our hands at Waipoua. We get two new weed species along the roadside every year from people dumping rubbish. We hand-weed that road twice a year because it's the point of entry to the forest.

Stephen King sees Te Roroa's continued and formalised involvement as the only sustainable way of protecting Waipoua Forest. He points out that much of the land under their Treaty claim has high conservation value:

The future of Waipoua is dependent on the settlement of the Te Roroa claim. If the settlement is just, there will be a good foundation for moving forward together.

As part of this foundation, the Waipoua Forest Trust and Te Roroa intend presenting a joint plan for a kauri national park once the Te Roroa Claim Settlement Bill becomes law.

Kauri forests for the future

Established in 1999, also as a Millennium project, the community-based Kauri 2000 Trust aims to restore the Coromandel kauri forests by planting nursery-grown kauri seedlings into carefully prepared, fertilised planting sites. The Trust has worked with the Department of Conservation and local authorities to select suitable sites on accessible public and privately covenanted land — mostly sites reverting to native scrub where few kauri seedlings are establishing naturally. The Trust is also exploring whether planting kauri seedlings on ridges would accelerate the establishment of natural stands in remote areas where most kauri seed trees were removed by logging or burning.

Volunteers for the Trust continue to plant kauri seedlings on thirty-four sites. Prime Minister Helen Clark planted the 10,000th tree in August 2001 with due ceremony, and the milestone of the 20,000th tree was reached in the 2006 planting season. A survey by Forest Research scientist David Bergin after the first two years showed that 80–90 percent of the seedlings planted in protective scrub cover were growing well.

A major factor in this early success has been the knowledge gained from Trust consultant Max Johnston's previous Forest Service experience with planting and tending kauri. The fate of those earlier plantings after the demise of the Forest Service in 1987 signals the immense challenge faced by the Trust in the decades ahead. When hundreds of hectares of planted kauri were abandoned, many untended plantings succumbed to competition from vigorous scrub and fern. Intensive tending of the Trust's plantings will be needed for at least three years — and probably beyond — if its enterprise and effort are to contribute 'towards a future where groves of these beautiful trees will once again dominate the forest canopy'.

At present, the Trust's focus is firmly on re-establishing a kauri presence in the Coromandel landscape. In the future, kauri forests planted or restored by groups like Kauri 2000 and the Waipoua Forest Trust could have a far wider significance. New Zealand is signatory to a growing number of international agreements such as the Montreal Process and the Convention on Biodiversity. These impose obligations for sustainable multi-purpose management of all forests — whether to protect biodiversity, preserve soil and water quality, retain social and cultural values, provide ecologically sustainable timber resources, or to contribute forest sinks that counteract carbon emissions. Under the Kyoto Protocol, forests planted since 1990 can yield carbon credits — long-lived diverse native plantings have greater potential to sequester carbon than short-rotation monocultural pine plantations. Such obligations and opportunities indicate that a paradigm shift may be needed in the way New Zealanders view kauri forests.

Present obligations, future opportunities

The long history of unsustainable exploitation of native forests and the legacy of the 1987 split between government conservation and commercial production fostered a strong public belief that native trees should not be used for timber production. Eighty-three percent of New Zealand's publicly owned native forests (5.2 million hectares) are legally preserved as conservation estate. Almost half the privately owned 1.1 million hectares of native forests have also been preserved by covenanting of various kinds. By 1987, most of New Zealand's timber needs and timber export income had already become reliant on exotic plantations of radiata pine, which were then progressively transferred from government ownership to private companies. The small amount of native timber still being harvested on private land became regulated by sustainable forest management permits and plans (SFMs) under the Forests Amendment Act 1993 and the requirements of the Resource Management Act 1991.

But the costs of compliance and helicopter-harvesting of quality native timber like kauri increased prices, so New Zealanders turned to cheaper imported tropical rainforest equivalents such as Fijian kauri and kwila. Since 1993, the unrestricted imports of timber and furniture have escalated several hundred percent in value (about $236 million value in 2006). Much of this is sourced from illegal logging operations in Malaysia and Indonesia. The ethics of conserving native forests at home while satisfying consumer demand by condoning non-sustainable felling of native forests in the Pacific and South-east Asia are dubious. The practice also runs counter to increasing international demands for the labelling of forest products and schemes, such as the independent Forest Stewardship Council's certification, which verify that forest management practices are sustainable.

International trends and obligations all point to New Zealand needing to look to its own native forests for future supplies of high-quality timber for high-value end uses. Under present legislation, the only native forests available for such timber production are privately owned. The challenge is to devise ecologically sustainable management systems that allow some timber production and use of other forest products while contributing to the conservation of biodiversity — a management concept that is poles apart from the narrowly focused, sustained timber yield goals of the twentieth century.

For New Zealand, developing such management systems will involve commitment and cooperation from government agencies and legislators, the conservation movement, scientists, and land-owners. Opportunities to adopt a holistic approach to the management of native forest have never been greater. With the removal of development subsidies that once encouraged farmers to clear regenerating forest, large areas of marginal farmland are now reverting to native scrub. Maori ownership of native forests, reverting scrublands, and cleared forest plantation land — already significant in remote rural areas — will increase as Treaty claims are resolved. Such areas all represent major opportunities to re-establish native forests and at the same time provide long-term rural employment and economic returns.

In recognition of these opportunities and the ultimate goal of achieving sustainable land use for New Zealand, Tane's Tree Trust was launched in 2001 by a group of committed experts and researchers with influential links to government. The Trust's aim is to encourage all land-owners to plant and manage native trees by taking on the task of pursuing funding, tax incentives, and reduced compliance costs. It coordinates research, field trials, and information sharing, and lobbies for any legislative and political changes needed to remove present obstacles to establishing an ecologically sustainable native forest industry. For kauri, such a future looks particularly promising. In the north, many reverting scrublands support vigorously regenerating kauri that would respond to management. Earlier Forest Service experiments, extended by Forest Research initiatives in the mid-1990s, have already provided a wealth of information on growing kauri. Well-managed kauri has excellent growth rates and its timber is unsurpassed for many high-value uses.

Envisage a potential northern landscape at the end of the twenty-first century. Planted stands of kauri rickers augment protected islands of natural vegetation. Representing the whole range of northern subtropical ecosystems, these protected islands shelter once-threatened native birds and other fauna. The high ongoing costs of restoring populations of icon species and protecting their habitats from invasive pests and weeds are covered by carbon credits. Legislative changes have allowed non-harvest Kyoto plantations of kauri to be established for that purpose on areas of conservation estate with low biodiversity values.

On private land, farmers earn good financial returns from a small-scale, ecologically sustainable harvest of maturing kauri trees in their fenced-off remnants of forest. All marginal land is planted in kauri and other native conifers — some registered for carbon sequestering, some to provide high-value timber for the future. Maori communities have economic security provided by native-timber harvesting certified by international agencies such as the Forest Stewardship Council — ensuring overseas markets. They are busy restoring culturally valued species for the use of future generations and developing a range of high-value forest health products based on traditional knowledge.

Despite the events that so dramatically changed the northern landscapes of New Zealand over a few hundred years of human history, the aging Tane Mahuta still holds up the sky at Waipoua. The ancient line of kauri — survivor of millions of years of cataclysmic change — operates on a time scale far longer than that of mere human history. With or without human intervention, kauri is sure to feature in the landscapes of New Zealand's future.

KEEPING CULTURE ALIVE

Renewing a childhood fascination with the big war canoe at Waitangi, Hec Busby (Te Rarawa and Ngati Kahu) learned the traditional skills of canoe making after *Nga-toki-matawhao-rua* was relaunched in 1973:

> *I'm a member of our Toi Maori committee, which deals with different traditions like weaving and carving. I'm trying to get everyone to pull together and demand that we carve a traditional waka [canoe] every five years to keep that knowledge and the culture alive, so that it's not lost.*

In 1990, the 150-year celebrations at Waitangi saw the revival of Waikato leader Te Puea Herangi's dream for a fleet of seven canoes to represent the major tribal groups. More than twenty big canoes were built, creating a magnificent fleet at Waitangi for the celebrations. Some of the northern canoes were made from kauri under Hec's supervision. But his real passion is double-hulled voyaging canoes.

Expert carver Hec Busby uses modern tools for building kauri canoes, mostly chainsaws and an adapted post peeler for hollowing out the hulls: 'If our ancestors had had these tools, they would have used them.'

The seventeen-metre long voyaging canoe, *Te Aurere*, was built from kauri felled in Herekino Forest. Completed by Hec and his team in 1989, the canoe has travelled over 30,000 nautical miles since its maiden voyage to Rarotonga in 1992. Hec — now in his seventies — has captained all but the outwards maiden voyage. The last voyage, to the 2000 South Pacific Arts Festival in New Caledonia, was seen by critics as a failure when *Te Aurere* was unable to reach Noumea in time, thwarted by adverse winds and currents. But Hec believes that nothing happens without reason. They made their landfall at the Ile des Pins, which he learned later had been the traditional landing place, making *Te Aurere* the first ocean-going canoe to land there for 700 years.

Permission to fell live kauri trees for canoes has to come from the Department of Conservation, after recommendation by a Maori cultural materials committee (Te Pataka o Taitokerau), set up by Northland Conservancy in 1990. Cutting live kauri in today's conservation climate is always going to be fraught with difficulties. Before Hec got permission to fell more kauri in Herekino Forest in 2000 for a new canoe to accompany *Te Aurere* to Rapanui (Easter Island) in 2008 (if funding is available), he had to push his case right through to the Prime Minister. The rare felling of living kauri for canoes is now the only purpose for which such permission is given.

Nearly a decade after the launch of *Te Aurere*, Hec Busby's weekend wananga (learning workshops) held to train young men in the traditional skills of canoe building, sailing, and navigation (using a star compass made of sticks stuck in the ground) have become formalised as the educational and cultural Kupe Waka Centre, built with Creative New Zealand funding support. The new double-hulled canoe will be completed in time to accompany *Te Aurere* to Rapanui:

> *We have no trouble getting crew. Something happens to those young men, that experience. It shows them how clever their ancestors were, restores some pride. They stick their chests out. That's why I keep going.*

Main References

General references

Adams, J. G. E., *Kauri: A King amongst Kings*, Auckland, Wilson and Horton, 1973.

Belich, J., *Making Peoples,* Auckland, Penguin Books, 1996.

Ell, G., *King Kauri: Tales and Traditions of the Kauri Country of New Zealand*, Auckland, The Bush Press, 1996.

Halkett, J. and Sale, E.V., *The World of the Kauri,* Auckland, Reed Methuen, 1986.

McKinnon, M. (ed.), *Bateman New Zealand Historical Atlas*, Auckland, David Bateman, 1997.

Reed, A. H., *The New Story of the Kauri,* Wellington, A. H. & A. W. Reed, 1964.

Sale, E. V., *Quest for the Kauri,* Wellington, A. H. & A. W. Reed, 1978.

Simpson, T. E., *Kauri to Radiata,* Auckland, Hodder & Stoughton, 1973.

CHAPTER 1

Ballara, A., 'Settlement Patterns in the Early European Phase of Maori Settlement', *Journal of the Polynesian Society*, 88 (2), 1979, pp. 199–213.

Best, E., *Forest Lore of the Maori,* Wellington, Government Printer, 1977 (1 e, 1944).

Best, E., *The Maori Canoe,* Wellington, Government Printer, 1977 (1 e, 1942).

Davidson, J., *The Prehistory of New Zealand,* Auckland, Longman Paul, 1984.

Davidson, J., 'Marks on a Landscape: Auckland's Volcanic Cones', in Wilson, J. (ed.), *The Past Today. Historic Places in New Zealand*, Auckland, Pacific Publishers, for New Zealand Historic Places Trust, 1987.

Davidson, J., 'The Paa Maori Revisited', *Journal of the Polynesian Society*, 96 (1), 1987, pp. 7–26.

Davidson, J., 'The Polynesian Foundation', in Rice, G. (ed.), *The Oxford History of New Zealand*, Auckland, Oxford University Press, 1992 (2 e).

Howearth, M. W., *The Mists of Time*, Auckland, Reed Publishing, 2003.

Leach, H. M., *1000 Years of Gardening in New Zealand,* Wellington, A. H. & A. W. Reed, 1984.

McGlone, M. S., 'Polynesian Deforestation of New Zealand: A Preliminary Synthesis', *Archaeology in Oceania*, 18, 1983, pp. 11–25.

McGlone, M. S., 'The Polynesian Settlement of New Zealand in Relation to Environmental and Biotic Changes', *New Zealand Journal of Ecology*, 12 (supplement), 1989, pp. 115–129.

Mead, H. M. and Grove, N., *Nga Pepeha a nga Tipuna,* Wellington, Victoria University Press, 2001.

Orbell, M., *Hawaiki: A New Approach to Maori Tradition*, Christchurch, University of Canterbury, 1985.

Orbell, M., *The Natural World of the Maori*, Auckland, Collins/Bateman, 1985.

Prickett, N. (ed.), *The First Thousand Years: Regional Perspectives on New Zealand Archaeology*, Palmerston North, Dunmore Press, 1982.

Simmons, D., *Maori Auckland*, Auckland, The Bush Press, 1987.

Stone, R. C. J., *From Tamaki-makau-rau to Auckland*, Auckland, Auckland University Press, 2001.

Sutton, D. G. (ed.), *The Archaeology of the Kainga*, (prefaces), Auckland, Auckland University Press, 1994 (2 e).

Taylor, R., *Te Ika a Maui*, London, 1870 (2 e).

Trotter, M. and McCulloch, B. (eds), *Unearthing New Zealand*, Wellington, Government Printing Office, 1989.

Waitangi Tribunal, *Wai 38: The Te Roroa Report Summaries*, 1992.

Wilson, J. (ed.), *From the Beginning: The Archaeology of the Maori*, Auckland, Penguin Books, 1987.

CHAPTER 2

Ahmed, M. and Ogden, J., 'Population Dynamics of the Emergent Conifer *Agathis australis* (D.Don) Lindl. (Kauri) in New Zealand.1. Population Structures and Tree Growth Rates in Mature Stands', *New Zealand Journal of Botany*, 25, 1987, pp. 217–229.

Burns, B. R. and Leathwick, J. R., 'Vegetation-Environment Relationships at Waipoua Forest, Northland, New Zealand', *New Zealand Journal of Botany*, 34, 1996, pp. 79–92.

Ecroyd, C.E., 'Biological Flora of New Zealand: 8. *Agathis australis*', *New Zealand Journal of Botany*, 20, 1982, pp. 17–26.

Enright, N. J., 'Litterfall Dynamics in a Mixed Conifer-Angiosperm Forest in Northern New Zealand', *Journal of Biogeography*, 26 (1), 1995, pp. 149–157.

Enright, N. J. et al., 'An Introduction', in Enright, N. J. and Hill, R. S. (eds), *The Southern Conifers*, Melbourne, Melbourne University Press, 1995.

Halkett, J., *Kauri Forest Management Review*, Auckland, Kauri Management Unit, New Zealand Forest Service, 1983.

Joint Campaign on Native Forests (NZ), 'Ecology of Kauri Forests', Appendix 2 in *Kauri 1984: A Submission on the Halkett 1983 Kauri Forest Management Review*, 1984.

Jones, W. G. et al. 1995, '*Wollemia nobilis*, a New Living Australian Genus and Species in the Araucariaceae', *Telopea*, 6 (2–3), 1984, pp. 173–176.
Kershaw, A. P. and McGlone, M. S., 'The Quaternary History of the Southern Conifers', Chapter 3 in Enright, N. J. and Hill, R. S. (eds), *The Southern Conifers*, Melbourne, Melbourne University Press, 1995.
McGregor, W. R., *The Waipoua Forest: The Last Virgin Kauri Forest of New Zealand*, Auckland, Able Dykes Ltd, 1948.
Ogden, J. et al., 'The Late Quaternary History of Kauri (*Agathis australis*) in New Zealand and Its Climatic Significance', *Journal of Biogeography*, 19, 1992, pp. 611–622.
Ogden, J. and Stewart, G. H., 'Community Dynamics of the New Zealand Conifers', Chapter 5 in Enright, N. J. and Hill, R. S. (eds), *The Southern Conifers*, Melbourne, Melbourne University Press, 1995.
Salmon, J. T., *The Native Trees of New Zealand,* Wellington, A.H. & A.W. Reed Ltd, 1980.
Silvester, W. B., 'The Biology of Kauri (*Agathis australis*) in New Zealand. II. Nitrogen Cycling in Four Kauri Forest Remnants', *New Zealand Journal of Botany*, 38, 2000, pp. 205–220.
Silvester, W. B. and Orchard, T. A., 'The Biology of Kauri (*Agathis australis*) in New Zealand. I. Production, Biomass, Carbon Storage, and Litter Fall in Four Kauri Forest Remnants', *New Zealand Journal of Botany*, 37, 1999, pp. 553–571.
Wardle, P., *The Vegetation of New Zealand*, Cambridge UK, Cambridge University Press, 1991.

CHAPTERS 3 & 4

Ballara, A., 'Hongi Hika', 'Ruatara', 'Te Pahi', in *The Dictionary of New Zealand Biography, The People of Many Peaks*, Vol 1, Wellington, Allen & Unwin / Department of Internal Affairs, 1991, pp. 15–18, 118–120, 217–219.
Beaglehole, J. C. (ed.), *The Journals of Captain James Cook on his Voyages of Discovery: Vol. I. The Voyage of the Endeavour 1768–1771*, Cambridge UK, Cambridge University Press, for the Hakluyt Society, 1968.
Cruise, R. A., *Journal of a Ten Months' Residence in New Zealand*, Christchurch, Kiwi Publishers, 1998 reprint [1824].
Davis, C. O., *The Life and Times of Patuone, the Celebrated Nga Puhi Chief*, Auckland, Field, 1876.
Earle, A., *A Narrative of a Nine Months' Residence in New Zealand*, Christchurch, Kiwi Publishers, 1998 reprint [1834].
Hawkins, C. W., *Convicts and Kauri*, Whakatane, Whakatane and District Historical Society, 1993.
Horsman, J., *The Coming of the Pakeha to Auckland Province*, Wellington, Hicks Smith, 1971.
Lee, J., *I Have Named It the Bay of Islands*, Auckland, Hodder & Stoughton, 1983.
Lee, J., *Hokianga*, Auckland, Hodder & Stoughton, 1987.
McNab, R. (ed.), *Historical Records of New Zealand*, Vols. 1 & 2, Wellington, 1908–1914.
Murray-Oliver, A., *Augustus Earle in New Zealand*, Christchurch, Whitcombe & Tombs, 1968.
Ollivier, I. (transcriber and translator), *Extracts from Journals Relating to the Visit to New Zealand in May–July 1772 of the French Ships Mascarin and Marquis de Castries under the Command of M. J. Marion du Fresne*, Wellington, Alexander Turnbull Library Endowment Trust: Indosuez New Zealand Ltd, 1985.
Ollivier, I. and Hingley, C. (transcribers and translators), *Extracts from Journals Relating to the Visit to New Zealand of the French Ship St Jean Baptiste in December 1769 under the Command of J. F. M. de Surville*, Wellington, Alexander Turnbull Library Endowment Trust: Indosuez New Zealand Ltd, 1987.
Owens, J. M. R., 'New Zealand before Annexation', in Rice, G. (ed.), *The Oxford History of New Zealand*, Auckland, Oxford University Press, 1992 (2 e).
Ryburn, W. R., *Tall Spars, Steamers and Gum: A History of the Kaipara from Early European Settlement, 1854–1947*, Auckland, Kaipara Publications, 1999.
Salmond, A., *Two Worlds*, Auckland, Viking, 1991.
Salmond, A., *Between Worlds*, Auckland, Viking, 1997.
Sherrin, R. A. and Wallace, J. H., *Early History of New Zealand*, Auckland, Brett, 1890.
Stone, R. C. J., *From Tamaki-makau-rau to Auckland*, Auckland, Auckland University Press, 2001.
Waitangi Tribunal, *Wai 38: The Te Roroa Report Summaries*, 1992.

CHAPTER 5

Bradley, E. K., *The Great Northern Wairoa*, Dargaville, 1973.
Buffet, P., 'Kauri Trade Linked Land and Sea', *New Zealand Forest Industries*, February 1990, pp. 17, 20–21, 24, 26.
Carr, E. A. and Carr, R. W., 'An Early Northern Wairoa Mill Manager', *Auckland–Waikato Historical Journal*, 76, 2000, pp. 18–25.
Cowan, J., 'Famous New Zealanders No 43: John Webster of Hokianga. The Adventures of a Pioneer', *The New Zealand Railways Magazine*, October 1936, pp. 17–23.
Eaddy, P. A., *'Neath Swaying Spars*, Auckland, Whitcombe & Tombs, 1936.
Hutchins, D. E., *Kauri Forests and Forests of the North and Forest Management*, New Zealand

Forestry, Part 1, Wellington, Government Printer, 1919.
Lee, J., *Hokianga*, Auckland, Hodder & Stoughton,1987.
Le Roy, A. E., 'The Great Barrier Island', *Journal of the Auckland–Waikato Historical Societies*, 32, April 1978, p.1.
Mackay, D., *Working the Kauri: A Social and Photographic History of New Zealand's Pioneer Kauri Bushmen*, Auckland, Random Century, 1991.
Robinson, N. C., 'Quiet Days Come to the Kaipara Harbour', *The Weekly News*, 30 July, 1947, p. 22.
Ryburn, W. R., *Tall Spars, Steamers and Gum: A History of the Kaipara from Early European Settlement, 1854–1947*, Auckland, Kaipara Publications,1999.
Stallworthy, J., *Early Northern Wairoa*, Dargaville, Wairoa Bell & Northern Advertiser Printing Works, 1916.
Stevenson, M. and Macdonald, W., 'Captain Ranulph Dacre', *Auckland–Waikato Historical Journal*, 37, September 1980, pp. 1–4.
Yarwood, V., *Between Coasts — from Kaipara to Kawau*, Auckland, David Bateman, 2000.

CHAPTER 6

Ballara, A., 'Tamati Waka Nene', in *The Dictionary of New Zealand Biography, The People of Many Peaks*, Vol 1, Wellington, Allen & Unwin / Department of Internal Affairs, 1991, pp. 56–59.
Barr, J., *The City of Auckland, New Zealand, 1840–1920*, Auckland, Whitcombe & Tombs, c.1922.
Blake, N., 'Fencible Houses Served Early Settlers Well', *Auckland–Waikato Historical Journal*, 36, April 1980, pp. 20–21.
Eaddy, P. A., *'Neath Swaying Spars*, Auckland, Whitcombe & Tombs, 1936.
Ell, G., *Colonial Style: Pioneer Buildings of New Zealand*, Auckland, The Bush Press, 1986.
Fowlds, G. M., *The Maori Association with the Volcanic Hills and Craters of the Auckland Isthmus*, Auckland, 1967.
Hawkins, C. W., *Out of Auckland*, Auckland, The Pelorus Press, 1960.
Hodgson, T. E. R., *The Heart of Colonial Auckland, 1865–1910,* Auckland, Random Century, 1992.
Horsman, J., *The Coming of the Pakeha to Auckland Province*, Wellington, Hicks Smith, 1971.
Jayne, V., 'The Pioneer Industry — Regions and Regulations', *New Zealand Forest Industries*, February 1990, pp. 31–33.
Keene, F., *Legacies in Kauri*, Whangarei, Northern Publishing Company, 1978.
De Latour, P., *A New Zealand Guide to Antique and Modern Furniture*, Auckland, Grantham House, 1993.
Lee, J., *I Have Named It the Bay of Islands*, Auckland, Hodder & Stoughton, 1983.
Mackay, D., *Working the Kauri: A Social and Photographic History of New Zealand's Pioneer Kauri Bushmen*, Auckland, Random Century, 1991.
Pigneguy, D., 'Te Aroha', *New Zealand Memories*, 3 (19), 1999, pp. 290–297.
Shaw, P., 'Dwelling Places. The New Zealand Villa: A Style That Has Never Lost Its Charm', *Pacific Way*, April 1991, pp. 40–43.
Simmons, D., *Maori Auckland*, Auckland, The Bush Press, 1987.
Stacpoole, J., *Colonial Architecture in New Zealand*, Wellington, A. H. & A. W. Reed, 1976.
Stewart, D., *New Zealand Villa Past and Present*, Auckland, Penguin Books (New Zealand), 1992.
Stone, R. C. J., *From Tamaki-makau-rau to Auckland*, Auckland, Auckland University Press, 2001.
Swainson, W., *Auckland, the Capital of New Zealand, and the Country Adjacent*, Auckland, J. Williamson, 1853.
Toomath, W., *Built in New Zealand*, Auckland, HarperCollins Publishers, 1996.

CHAPTER 7

Ballara, A., 'Te Horeta', in *The Dictionary of New Zealand Biography, The People of Many Peaks*, Vol 1, Wellington, Allen & Unwin / Department of Internal Affairs, 1991, pp. 173–175.
Firth, R. W., *The Kauri Gum Industry: Some Economic Aspects*, unpublished MA thesis, Auckland, Auckland University College, University of New Zealand, 1922.
Hargreaves. R. P., 'The Maori Agriculture of the Auckland Province in the Mid-Nineteenth Century', *Journal of the Polynesian Society*, 68, 1959, pp. 61–79.
Hayward, B. W., *Kauri Gum and the Gumdiggers: A Pictorial History of The Kauri Gum Industry in New Zealand*, Auckland, Lodestar Press, 1982.
Lee, J., *Hokianga*, Auckland, Hodder & Stoughton, 1987.
McNeill, J., 'Northland's Buried Treasure', *New Zealand Geographic*, 10, 1991, pp. 18–45.
Ngoungou, Mrs, 'My Life among the Maori', first published in *The Sun*, Auckland, 27 July 1929, reprinted *Historical Review*, 14 (1), March 1996.
Parker, K., *Kaitaia — Portraits from the Past: 1900–39*, Kaitaia, Bridgewater Publications, 1999.
Reed, A. H., *The Gumdiggers: The Story of Kauri Gum*, Wellington, A. H. & A. W. Reed, 1972.

Smith, A. W., *The Development of the Kauri-Gum Industry and Its Role in the Economy of Northland, New Zealand*, Washington USA, unpublished PhD thesis for the University of Washington (copy held at Otamatea Kauri Museum, Matakohe), 1952.

Trlin, A. D., *Now Respected Once Despised: Yugoslavs in New Zealand*, Palmerston North, The Dunmore Press, 1979.

Wagener, R., *The Gumfields of Aupouri*, Kaitaia, 1977.

Wagener, R., *The 'Desart' Shore*, Pukenui, 1983.

Waitangi Tribunal, *Wai 38: The Te Roroa Report Summaries*, 1992.

CHAPTER 8

Bell, W. A., 'Life in a Timber Kauri Camp', *Journal of the Auckland Historical Society*, 6, April 1965, pp. 13–16.

Buffet, P., 'Kauri Trade Linked Land and Sea', *New Zealand Forest Industries*, February 1990, pp. 17, 20–21, 24, 26.

Mackay, D., *Working the Kauri: A Social and Photographic History of New Zealand's Pioneer Kauri Bushmen*, Auckland, Random Century, 1991.

Pearson, D., 'Kauri Driving Dams: Heritage in Decay', *Historic Places*, 34, September 1991, pp. 27–29.

CHAPTER 9

Adams, J. G. E., *Kauri: A King amongst Kings*, Auckland, Wilson and Horton, 1973.

Bellingham, M., 'What Future for Kauri?', *Forest & Bird*, 15 (3), 1984, pp. 14–17.

Best, H. A. and Bellingham, P. J., *A Detailed Habitat Study of North Island Kokako in Puketi Forest, Northland*, Department of Conservation Science and Research Report, 103, 1991.

Halkett, J. C., *Kauri Forest Management Review*, Auckland, Kauri Management Unit, New Zealand Forest Service, 1983.

Joint Campaign on Native Forests (NZ), *A Submission on the Halkett 1983 Kauri Forest Management Review*, 1984.

McGregor, W. R., *The Waipoua Forest: The Last Virgin Kauri Forest of New Zealand*. Auckland, Able Dykes Ltd, 1948.

McLean, M., *The Garden of New Zealand*, Department of Conservation Science and Research Report, 76, 1990.

New Zealand Forest Service, *Waipoua Kauri Forest*, New Zealand Forest Service Information Series, 14, 1952.

Ogle, D., *Beyond the Twenty-Foot Stump*, Russell, Bay of Islands, Northland Historical Publications Society, 1998.

Thom, D., *Heritage: The Parks of the People*, Auckland, Lansdowne Press, 1987.

Waitangi Tribunal, *Wai 38: The Te Roroa Report Summaries*, 1992.

Yarwood, V., 'Kauri', *New Zealand Geographic*, 2, 1989, pp. 86–111.

CHAPTER 10

Barton, I., 'Managing Kauri on the Farm. Parts 1–3', *New Zealand Tree Grower*, 15 (4), November 1994, pp. 27–28, 16 (3), August 1995, pp. 35–37, 17 (2), May 1996, pp. 31–35.

Bergin, D. O., 'Performance of the First Two Years of Kauri Planting Undertaken by the Kauri 2000 Trust, Coromandel Peninsula', Rotorua, Forest Research, 2002.

Best, H. A. and Bellingham, P. J., *A Detailed Habitat Study of North Island Kokako in Puketi Forest, Northland*, Department of Conservation Science and Research Report, 103, 1991.

Ell, G., 'Our Kauri Heritage: A National Park for the North', *Forest & Bird*, No 248, May 1988, pp. 4–7.

Ell, G., 'What Happened to the Kauri National Park?', *Forest & Bird*, No 281, August 1994, pp. 28–31.

MacGibbon, R. et al., *Proceedings of the Launch of Tane's Tree Trust*, Waiuku, Tane's Tree Trust, 2002.

Mikaere, B., 'Year of the Waka', *New Zealand Geographic*, 5, January–March 1990, pp. 8–29.

New Zealand Conservation Authority, *Investigation into the Proposal for a Kauri National Park in Northland: Interim Report*. Wellington, New Zealand Conservation Authority, 1995.

Northland Conservancy, *Northland Kauri National Park Proposal: Public Discussion Paper*, Whangarei, Department of Conservation, 1990.

Northland Conservancy, *Northland Kauri National Park Investigation: Report to the New Zealand Conservation Authority*. Whangarei, Department of Conservation, 1992.

Northland Conservancy, *Conservation Management Strategy: Northland Conservancy 1999–2009*, Whangarei, Department of Conservation, 1998.

Norton, D., 'Sustainable Forest Management in New Zealand', in Lindenmayer, D. B. and Franklin, J. F. (eds), *Towards Forest Sustainability*, Melbourne, CSIRO Publishing, 2003.

O'Connor, D. (Chairperson), *A Sustainable Future for our Indigenous Forests*, Report of the Primary Production Committee, Wellington, New Zealand House of Representatives, 2002.

Index

Page numbers in italic indicate illustrations.